# ABRAHAM, JOSEPH, AND MOSES IN EGYPT:

BEING A COURSE OF LECTURES DELIVERED BEFORE
THE THEOLOGICAL SEMINARY, PRINCETON,
NEW JERSEY.

BY

REV. ALFRED H. KELLOGG, D.D.,

OF PHILADELPHIA,

MEMBER OF "VICTORIA INSTITUTE," ETC., ETC.

ISBN: 978-1-63923-658-9

Printed: January 2023

Published and Distributed By:
Lushena Books
607 Country Club Drive, Unit E
Bensenville, IL 60106
www.lushenabks.com

ISBN: 978-1-63923-658-9

# NOTE.

—o—

THE time has not arrived for me to re-write these Lectures for a revised edition, but I wish to make a correction or two that crept into the volume, and to make some additions—more particularly to the Lectures on "Joseph," and the "Exodus Pharaoh"—that may bring the volume up to date. I will be obliged if those who receive this paper will kindly insert it in their copy of my book.

ALFRED H. KELLOGG.

*April,* 1892.

# I.—ERRATA.

(1) The Scripture reference on p. 126 should be *Exodus* xi. 5.

(2) Misled by statements of Dr. Birch in "Records of the Past" and Dr. Brugsch in his "History," I state on p. 23 that the Tanis tablet is "at present in the Boulak Museum." This is not so. Too late for any alteration in the text, I learned that Mariette, after discovering it at Tanis, being unable to carry it away, and wishing to preserve it from use for building purposes or other injury at the hands of the natives, carefully copied its inscriptions and then re-buried it *in situ*. It has not been re-discovered. (See Note.)

(3) The point raised in the Essay-appendix is no longer in dispute, so that in the next edition that Essay will be omitted.

# II.—ADDENDA.

[NOTE.—I have no changes to make in Lectures I., II., and IV.]

## LECTURE III.

As to Joseph's place in Egypt, I find additional reasons for the main contentions of the lecture.

Mr. Tomkins thinks my "chronology untenable," but Mr. Tomkins was writing to support his own contention, which regards Joseph's Pharaoh as a Shepherd King. I know that Mr. Naville agrees with him on this point, but neither of them has seriously attacked the question. I would be grateful if either of them would draw up a chronological scheme that would include all the monumental elements as to the order of succession and regnal periods of the era, and then would attempt to harmonise such a definite chronology with the numerous data of Genesis and Exodus, as well as with what we may call coincidences in thought and expression gathered from both the Scripture and the Egyptian traditions. I am sure that then neither they, nor even Herr Brugsch with his fertile imagination, would again attempt the task of pushing back Joseph into the Shepherd era.

My main contentions in the lecture are (1), that Joseph's Pharaoh belonged to a *native* dynasty; and (2), that he was one of the *Eighteenth* dynasty Kings.

I went further, and thought myself justified in picking out two great Kings of that dynasty (according as one adopted a longer or shorter Egyptian chronology)—to wit, Thothmes III. and Amenophis III., either of whose reigns, as respects length and other particulars, could satisfy the requirements of the Genesis-story.

Of course, certainty and perfect accuracy were then as now out of the question; but whatever one may affirm, it has never yet been proven that either the longer or the shorter chronology in dispute is "untenable." I would like to see an offered scheme that is more tenable.

There are a number of difficulties requiring explanation on the part of those

struggle took place. Genesis affirms that Joseph himself continued to live in Egypt eighty years after his elevation and died there. The same is true of Joseph's brethren and their descendants. Why, we ask, were the Hebrews passed by and not expelled by a dynasty that could have had no sympathy with them on any ground and that must have hated them as both foreigners and Shepherds?

It will not do to say that at the period of the expulsion they were yet few in number, and therefore an unimportant element, for that would mean a *very* short period between the Apepi of Joseph and Aahmes, and Joseph's life would then overlap the new dynasty for a considerable time—all of which would suggest difficulties equally great. My own contention presents no difficulty whatever on this point.

(2) The background of the Hebrew story is admitted to be Egyptian to the core. And though it is affirmed that this would be equally true if Joseph's Pharaoh were a Shepherd, inasmuch as the Shepherds became completely Egyptianised, I cannot help feeling that the coincidences with Egyptian thought and expression that Mr. Tomkins notices would suggest to most readers that Joseph's Pharaoh was " to the manner born." It is too natural and precise and formal an Egyptian portrait to belong to a foreigner.

The composition of the names of Joseph's prison-keeper and wife and father-in law have been very gratuitously affirmed by Brugsch (in the interest of the so-called higher criticism) as proof of the late composition of Genesis— as late on, in fact, as the era of the Twenty-second dynasty. But Mr. Tomkins, in this instance, has proved that the veteran Egyptologist allowed his zeal to run away with his judgment ; for just such composition of proper names as those in question *are found* in the very dynasty to which we believe Joseph's Pharaoh belonged, and, what is of still greater interest, in the very reign of Thothmes III., one of the two kings of that dynasty that it is possible to think of as a Pharaoh of Joseph.

I may add that it is a slight but curious circumstance that the first time the word "Aperu " (*i.e.*, " Hebrew ") is found on an Egyptian record is in the reign of this same Thothmes, and in an honourable connection. It was brought to light by the late Mr. Goodwin. It is apparently a royal order for a Hebrew aide-de-camp to attend His Majesty. The fact is certainly worth noting, because, as is evident all through the Genesis-story, Joseph and his brethren and descendants were known to the Egyptians distinctively as " Hebrews." (See Gen. xxxix. 14, xl. 15, xli. 12, xliii. 32, &c.)

(3) Take the phrase, " The new king that knew not Joseph," which, all admit, refers to the rise of the Nineteenth dynasty. Let me ask, Would not the phrase have more point if Joseph's elevation occurred in the dynasty immediately preceding, than in one before that ? The phrase would be equally true of Aahmes and his successors (if Joseph lived under the Shepherds), and could easily justify any possible ill-treatment of the Hebrews by them. And yet the native dynasty headed by Aahmes did not expel the Hebrews. As far as is known, they were not ill-treated. The *Nineteenth* dynasty was the dynasty of the oppressors.

(4) Considerable interest has been lately aroused by Mr. Wilbour's discovery

Unfortunately the Pharaoh's name in whose era the famine is said to have occurred, is, in both places where it is met, undecipherable—at least, with certainty. Brugsch, deciding from photographs sent to him, is very positive that the name is to be identified with Manetho's "Tosorthros" of the latter half of the Third dynasty. On the contrary, the discoverer and Mr. Sayce are reported as reading all three of the signs composing the name differently, albeit their reading allows of no identification with any known Pharaoh. The tablet itself, it is agreed, dates from a Ptolemaic or even Roman period.

Renouf regards the tablet as "evidently a pious fraud, drawn up for the purpose of furnishing ancient precedent for recent practice"; though he also regards the stone "as not the less interesting, as showing that there was a tradition in Egyptian that there had, at some early date, been a period of severe distress through a famine which had lasted for seven years."

The name, however, *as Brugsch reads it*, is interesting from another point of view. He identifies it with one of two kings of the Third dynasty—an era which is, of course, long anterior to the time of Joseph's famine. But Brugsch himself goes into considerable detail to show with what freedom later Pharaohs referred to the heroes of the past as their ancestors. Many "pious frauds," as Renouf calls them, were practised in referring to "ancient precedents for recent practice." The object of this particular tablet, *e.g.*, was to ensure the continued payment to the "great God of the cataracts" of what may be called tithes of all produce, basing the claim on an ancient royal decree that is said to have been made in consequence of a seven years' famine that occurred in the Pharaoh's reign; and it is of interest to note that a dream of the Pharaoh is referred to. It cannot be doubted that the story of the tablet is at least a reminiscence of an actual occurrence. The point, however, that seems to be worth stating refers to the name chosen by the author of the tablet as the Pharaoh of the famine. As stated, the name is almost beyond decipherment. Still, one of the three signs is most probably (Brugsch is positive about it) "tser" or "ser."

Now, it is curious that the only known royal names that contain this special sign are the two Pharaohs of the Third dynasty (to one of which Brugsch assigns the Pharaoh of the famine), and two Pharaohs of the *Eighteenth* dynasty—viz., Horus, the last king of that dynasty, and Amenophis I., the grandfather of Thothmes III. It is also curious that the latter's distinctive cartouche has but three signs (Ra *ser* Ka). It may be, therefore, that the real famine Pharaoh of the tablet was Amenophis I., of the Eighteenth dynasty, but to the author of the tablet he may not have seemed ancient enough for a precedent. Scanning the list of the more ancient heroes, he found another "ser," and in this way, by a "pious fraud," the famine Pharaoh may have been relegated to the Third dynasty.

To be sure the recurrence of the sign referred to in Dynasty XVIII., may be the merest coincidence and without importance. I don't wish this paragraph to be taken too seriously. And yet it is curious to observe how everything, circumstances most trivial as most important, would suggest Dynasty XVIII., never a Shepherd era for Joseph's Pharaoh.

to say, have been in such haste to commit themselves to this view, that the impression has been left on the public mind that he is really so. From this view I most earnestly dissent, and my appeal is to the testimony of the monuments.

I see no reason to change the main contentions of my lecture on this point. Indeed, I am more confirmed than ever in the conviction that whoever the Exodus Pharaoh was, he was not, nor *could he be*, the son of Rameses II. To mention but one argument of many, and an unanswerable one, I would draw special attention to the note found on page 126, particularly the latter part of it.

It is clear from the Scripture story, that the firstborn son and heir of the Exodus Pharaoh *died on the eve of the Exodus*—an event which, indeed, was the immediate occasion of the permission (or rather command) to the Hebrews to depart. Any Pharaoh, therefore, to be the Exodus Pharaoh, must answer to this crucial test. That being so, it can be confidently affirmed that the son of Rameses II. cannot have been the Exodus Pharaoh, for *his* son and heir was not only associated with his father on the throne during the latter part of his reign, but, as the monuments prove, *survived his father* and continued to reign alone for at least two years.* The son of Mineptah, therefore, who "sat upon the throne" with his father, did *not die*, as the Bible story would require, if his father was the Exodus Pharaoh. He lived to succeed him.

This single fact should put a stop to the confident way in which so many nowadays refer to the son of Rameses II. as the Exodus Pharaoh—softened sometimes by the phrase "The *supposed* Pharaoh of the Exodus." If monumental testimony is worth anything, he *could not* have been such.

If asked who then was the Exodus Pharaoh, I can only refer to my Lecture VI. That lecture takes for granted the contention of Lecture V., viz.: that the disaster that brought Dynasty XIX. to a collapse—such a collapse that for "many years Egypt was in confusion" (as the great Harris Papyrus puts it)—was in very truth the Exodus of the Hebrews. That contention has never been disproved. If the *monumental* "Exodus" and the *Hebrew* Exodus were not one and the same event, then the coincidence of two such events in that part of Dynasty XIX. is truly remarkable and inexplicable.

But my Lecture VI. takes it for granted that the two were one, and accordingly my main contention in Lecture VI. is, that whoever the Exodus Pharaoh was, he must have been *the last Pharaoh* of Dynasty XIX.

At the time of my lectures, it however remained uncertain who it was that brought the dynasty to a close. And I am sorry to say that the last word on this point has not yet been spoken. It remains uncertain still. The occasion of the uncertainty is given in detail in my Lecture VI. In brief it is this— that notwithstanding the monumental testimony that affirms that Seti II. (Mineptah's son) succeeded his father, nay, was associated with him previous to his death, there is a difficulty as to this point met with in the tomb of

Siptah,* which seems to teach that Seti II. *succeeded Siptah!* This latter point doubtless led Maspero to adopt Seti II. as his Exodus Pharaoh. But the monumental testimony as to Seti's succeeding his father Mineptah is simply incontrovertible, and accordingly at the date of my lectures, taking that for granted, I tried to explain (or explain away) the counter-testimony (apparently) of Siptah's tomb (see the latter half of the Lecture) and was strongly inclined to close the dynasty with Siptah.

I have come to think, however, that the problem may be solved in another way, *i.e.*, by accepting both monumental affirmations, and admit that Seti II. succeeded both his father, Mineptah (which was a fact beyond doubt), and later on Siptah also, as Siptah's tomb appears to teach. This may appear a contradiction, but it can be harmonised by the supposition that the only other two Pharaohs yielded by the monuments of the period, viz., Amenmes and Siptah, interrupted the reign of·Seti II. At any rate, such a supposition contradicts no monumental fact. It is undoubtedly true (as intimated) that Seti II. succeeded Mineptah, his father. There is mention made of his second year, and then there is silence. But his tomb, scarcely more than begun, shows that the peace which characterised his reign at the beginning did not last long—that it came to an abrupt end. Then, too, it is possible that the tradition of a Mineptah's flight to Ethiopia with his young son, and subsequent return, may refer to this Seti II. (who was a "Mineptah," as well as his father). The flight was occasioned by a revolt headed by rival Pharaohs. At any rate, the evidence of Siptah's tomb (if it be insisted upon) would show that after the brief reigns of Amenmes and Siptah, Seti II. resumed his reign. He may have wrested the crown from Siptah, or he may have been recalled after Siptah's death. The facts of Siptah's tomb would argue (on any hypothesis) an intended indignity to one who, at best, probably reigned only as husband to his queen, who was queen by an incontestible title.

If the supposition be allowed, of course it follows that Maspero was justified in adopting Seti II. as the Exodus Pharaoh.

On the other hand, there is much to be said in favour of closing the dynasty with Siptah (see the details in my lecture). At this writing, therefore, the question remains an open one. But two results must be clear:—(1) The Exodus Pharaoh could not be Mineptah, son of Rameses II. (2) He must have been the last Pharaoh of the dynasty, and, therefore, either Seti II. or Siptah, according to the order of succession adopted for the three kings who followed the son of Rameses II. We have simply to wait patiently for some "find" that will clear up the mystery.

---

* The reference is to the way in which in Siptah's tomb a cartouche (which it is taken for granted is that of Seti II.) is superimposed upon Siptah's cartouche. For, as appears, Siptah's tomb was twice usurped—first by Seti II. (if it be his cartouche) and later on by Setnekht, founder of Dynasty XX.

I state in my lecture that the superimposed cartouche may not have been that of the Second Seti, but the cartouche of another Seti, who is represented in a tomb-picture as

# PREFACE.

THE purpose of this course of lectures is to ascertain, if possible, the position of Abraham, Joseph and Moses in Egypt's history.

It would be premature to attempt to fix the date of the era in the world's chronology, although many such attempts have been made. The first date in Egypt's history that can be dated with precision is as late on as Dynasty XXVI. The chronology of what goes before is purely conjectural, and depends on the estimates made of the gaps and uncertain time-elements, that persistently remain such.

All that is possible at present is to reconstruct such periods (longer or shorter) as can be fairly well recovered from the monuments, and to wait patiently for further "finds," that may serve to connect these together.

Accordingly, no attempt has been made to fix the chronology of our period absolutely, but relatively to its own contents. There are serious gaps even in the period discussed in the lectures; and the utmost that can be claimed is that parts of it have been made out with some degree of certainty and that the gaps have become more clearly defined. Where so much is necessarily hypothetical, it seems reasonable to enter a caveat against the tendency of the times unduly to prolong Egypt's chronology. There certainly is no need of writing about " centuries" for intervals, when decades would answer as well.

The lectures are humbly submitted simply as a study in the comparative chronology of Egypt's monuments and the Bible tradition, — not in any dogmatic spirit, but as a tentative effort, looking to the harmony of the two sources of history. Whatever may be thought of the positions assumed in any one lecture, the author would venture to ask that judgment · may be suspended until the six lectures are read through. The argument of the one part will be found to be supported by the argument of another part and the connection of the whole. The lectures are published with the hope that they will be accepted in the spirit in which they are conceived, and in the sure confidence that ultimately perfect harmony will be discovered between the chronological indications of the monuments and the data of Holy Scripture.

*March,* 1887.

# SUMMARY OF THE LECTURES.

## LECTURE I.

LECTURE II.

LECTURE III.

DYNASTIC LIST XII.-XX.

| Dynasty XII. | Dynasty XVII. |
|---|---|
| AMENEMHAT I. | (Native Line.)        (Shepherds.) |
| USERTESEN I. | RASEKENEN (TA-AA)    I. . . . . APEPI. (61) |
| AMENEMHAT II. | RASEKENEN (TA-AA-AA)  II. |
| USERTESEN II. | RASEKENEN (TA-AA-KEN) III. |
| USERTESEN III. | KAMES. |
| AMENEMHAT III. | |
| AMENEMHAT IV. | **Dynasty XVIII.** |
| SEBEKNEFERUKA. | AAHMES. |
| | AMENHOTEP I. |
| **Dynasty XIII. et cet.** | THOTHMES I. |
| SEBEKHOTEP I. | THOTHMES II.    & HATASU. |
| . . . . . . . . . . | THOTHMES III. |
| | AMENHOTEP II |

In List of THOTHMES III.

| Tu.Paps. | |
|---|---|
| No. 6. | S'ANKHABRA. |
| . . . . . . . . . . | |
| No. 16. | SEBEKHOTEP III. |
| . . . . . . . . . . | |
| No. 21. | SEBEKHOTEP IV. |
| . . . . . . . . . . | |
| No. 22. | NEFERHOTEP. |
| . . . . . . . . . . | |
| No. 24. | SEBEKHOTEP V. |
| ? | |
| No. 26. | SEBEKHOTEP VI. |
| No. 27. | SEBEKHOTEP VII. |
| . . . . . . . . . . | |
| No. 45. | MERKAURA. |

. . . . . . . . . .
. . . . . . . . . .
. . . . . . . . . .
. . . . . . . . . .
. . . . . . . . . .

**Dynasty XVIII.** (continued)

THOTHMES IV.
AMENHOTEP III.
AMENHOTEP IV. (Khuenaten).
SA'ANEKHT.
TUT'ANKHAMEN.
AI.
HORUS.

**Dynasty XIX.**

RAMESES I.
SETI I. (Mineptah I.).
RAMESES II. (Miamen).
MINEPTAH (II. Hotephima).
SETI II. (Mineptah III.).
AMENMES.
SIPTAH (Mineptah IV.) & TAUSER.

**Dynasty XX.**

SETNEKHT.
RAMESES III.
RAMESES IV. et cet.

# ABRAHAM, JOSEPH, AND MOSES IN EGYPT.

## LECTURE I.

### CHRONOLOGY OF THE EGYPTIAN DYNASTIES, XII.-XX.

THERE are but two sources for the reconstruction of Egyptian chronology, — (1) the monuments, and (2) the traditions of Manetho and other ancient authors. To be sure, an appeal may subsequently be made to certain Scripture time-indications, which as far as they go furnish corroborative proof of results reached ; but the sacred writer does not complete the story of Egypt, as that was not Moses' object.

The statements of the monuments are of course final as far as they go, though unfortunately these up to now cover but parts of our period.

As to the traditions of Manetho and other ancient authors, criticism has to deal with these very carefully, — one might say, sometimes severely. The statements of Greek and Latin authors, which up to quite recently formed the basis of our Egyptian histories, are proven by the monuments to be of little

value.  Professor Sayce is particularly severe on
Herodotus,[1] affirming " that modern research obliges
us to indorse the judgment passed upon Herodotus
almost as soon as his History was published, and that
it is not only untrustworthy, but unveracious."

Did we but possess the original work of Manetho
the Egyptian priest, who at the instance of Ptolemy
Philadelphus wrote in Greek a history of his people
professedly drawn from the monuments, it would
doubtless prove invaluable for our purpose.  Unfortunately, it has survived only in some extracts and
summaries incorporated in the works of Josephus
and of some Christian writers, particularly Africanus
and Eusebius, and later on of Syncellus.[2]

With great industry and zeal Lepsius collected
together, in his " Tables of Manetho Sources," [3] the
historical data of these extracts, adding thereto every
tradition alleged to have been Manetho's; so that a
very fair idea of their value may be obtained by
comparing the lists.  The comparison will be sure to
convince any one that Chabas' estimate was just,
though severe, when, referring to the extreme confusion of the lists, he affirmed that without the assistance of the monuments it would be an impossible
task to gather from them what Manetho really did

---

[1] Ancient Empires of the East, — Preface, p. xxii.

[2] Julius Africanus died A. D. 232 ; Eusebius Pamphili of Cæsarea, A. D.
270-340.  George Syncellus lived in the eighth century.  His work was a
compilation from other abbreviators.

[3] They form the middle section of the " Königsbuch," Berlin, 1858.

say. He adds: " All the versions bear traces of in-
terpolations or of falsifications." [1]

It is certainly, therefore, not without reason that
greatest reserve should be exercised in quoting from
them, and especially in basing an argument upon
them. The one fact, however, that can be attributed
to Manetho beyond any doubt is his division of
Egypt's history into Dynasties, or Houses, — a division which, however it be interpreted in its details, is
of greatest convenience in handling the narrative.

It must not be inferred from what has been said
that the Manetho lists are valueless, or even of little
worth. The lists, and particularly his dynastic divisions, have proven an invaluable help in locating,
with more or less of certainty, the scattered names
gathered from the monuments. Still, in any contro-
versy between the two sources of reconstruction, a
monumental fact or date must be accepted as final.
Certainty therefore, in the present inquiry, will
mean certainty as assured by monumental indications. It is only when these fail that the Manetho
indications may be accepted, though even then simply as a temporary bridge over a chasm.

Advancing to our task, — the reconstruction of
the chronology of the period covered by Dynasties
XII.–XX., — that of Dynasty XII. need not Chronology
of Dynasty
detain us long. Its founder was one Ame- XII.
nemhat I., who mounted the throne after a war of

---

[1] Les Pasteurs (Amsterdam, 1868), p. 14.

succession, and became the ancestor of a notable series of kings, some of whom were venerated in the
latest era. The order of succession and the regnal
periods of its eight sovereigns have been fairly well
recovered from the monuments, though there remains an element of uncertainty as to the exact
time-period of the Dynasty arising from lack of monumental information as to the time that should be
allowed for the associated reigns of one or two of
the Pharaohs. The reigns of these Amenemhats
and Usertesens furnished Egypt with a strong and
beneficent government. During the first six reigns
Egypt greatly prospered. Nubia was conquered,
and the name "Cush" first appears on the monuments. The mines of the Sinaitic Peninsula were
occupied and worked. Great public works were ex-
ecuted, looking to the regulation of the Nile inun-
dations and the artificial irrigation of the country.
Architecture, painting, sculpture, and literature divided the attention of these Pharaohs, equally skilled
in the arts of peace and of war. But the Dynasty
seems to have suddenly collapsed; for the last two
reigns — a brother and a sister — were brief (but
nine and four years respectively), betokening trouble
of some kind. At any rate, the brilliant Dynasty,
after ruling Egypt for about 170 years, came to an
end.[1]

---

[1] Both Maspero (in his "Histoire Ancienne," p. 98, note 5) and Brugsch
(in his "History of Egypt," vol. i. p. 120) have discussed the chronology of
this Dynasty, and both make the total somewhat larger, not allowing suf-

Leaving now Dynasty XII., and passing over for the present the obscurer part of our period, — Dynasties XIII.–XVII., — we would next con- Chronology of Dynasty sider Dynasty XVIII. XVIII.

The Manetho lists covering Dynasty XVIII. are in a state of great confusion. Even from a monumental point of view, the Dynasty is full of problems. Still, it is possible to recover from the monuments the order of succession with but few elements of uncertainty, and to gather a fair idea of the dynastic period.

Its founder was one Aahmes, Egypt's liberator from the Shepherds, who was succeeded by his son Amenophis I., and he by his son Thothmes I. Thothmes I. was succeeded by three of his children, — a daughter and two sons, as they are generally regarded. The first of them, Thothmes II., married his sister, and was completely dominated by her, she being the virtual ruler, — the masculine Queen Hatasu. The rule of her husband-brother did not last long, and it ended obscurely. Hatasu succeeded, nominally as Regent to her younger brother, but for a time at least she assumed the style and even the dress of a king, ruling as such some fifteen years, and only allowing the young Thothmes to be associated with her when

ficient for the associated parts of the later reigns. The amount of overlapping in the earlier four reigns can be gathered from the monuments; but this is not true of the later reigns, and forms an element of uncertainty. The Turin Papyrus makes the sum 213 years by counting, though with a slight error, the regnal periods and without allowance for any overlapping. The Manetho lists make the period 168, — a number probably much nearer the truth. The dynastic period adopted in the text is probably quite correct.

it could no longer be avoided. Her reign, though brilliant, was resented by Thothmes III. He dishonored her monuments and ignored her rule, dating his own reign from the date of his brother's death.

Egyptologists are now pretty well agreed that eighty-one years would be ample to cover the period from the accession of Aahmes to the first year of Thothmes III.

The monuments yield the period of the latter's reign to a day. It was fifty-four years, less about a month.[1] The monuments yield but seven years each to his two successors, Amenophis II. and Thothmes IV., but assign to the next Pharaoh, Amenophis III., a reign of some thirty-six years. They also yield the twelfth year for his son Amenophis IV., or Khuenaten, though it is probable that he survived for another year.

The rest of the Dynasty is differently treated by different scholars. It may suffice to say that monumental data would indicate that only what may be called a long generation really intervened between Amenophis III. and Seti I. of the succeeding Dynasty, — the intervening six Pharaohs (Amenophis IV., the three Heretical Kings so-called, Horus the Reactionary, and Rameses I.) being contemporaries. The limits of uncertainty of this part of the Dynasty will be more apparent in a later lecture, and need not detain us now.

[1] Brugsch's History, vol. i. p. 314.

We may then at once consider Dynasty XIX.

In the case of this Dynasty, what has been said respecting the confusion attaching to the Manetho lists and the need of monumental information to set matters right, will be well illustrated. Chronology of Dynasty XIX. The annexed diagram comprises six of the Manetho lists of the Dynasty given by Lepsius in his " Tables," the first of which we may for the moment regard as the standard Manetho, and compare therewith the other five. The comparison will show how impossible it would be, with Manetho alone, to reconstruct either the order of succession or the regnal periods of this Dynasty. It will be observed how confusion attaches to even the dynastic division in Lists IV. and V., these beginning Dynasty XIX. with an interpolated " Sethos " instead of with the " Armaïs " of the other lists, Armaïs being relegated by them to the previous Dynasty.

In this particular instance it is fortunately possible from monumental indications, tabulated in the last column, to reconstruct with a good degree of certainty the earlier two-thirds of the Dynasty and the latter third with a good degree of probability. In this case, therefore, the monuments show how the Manetho lists need to be corrected. We have indicated it in the diagram by putting in italics the parts that must be omitted altogether, and by enclosing the parts that must be transposed and placed after Sethos I. But even when this has been done, criticism would next have to deal severely with the regnal periods of the lists.

The monuments now make it certain that Dynasty XIX. should be headed by Rameses I., and that he should be followed by Seti I., Rameses II., and Mineptah. The further order of succession is not quite so sure, there being some uncertainty as to whether the order should be that adopted in the diagram, or whether Seti II. should be made to follow Siptah and thus end the Dynasty. There is also some uncertainty as to the regnal periods of the seven Pharaohs. This is indicated, in the monumental column of the diagram, by putting in parentheses the periods claimed by some for what they consider good reasons, the other numbers being the years yielded by the monuments.

We are thus brought to the middle section of our period, — that beginning with Dynasty XIII. and Chronology ending with Dynasty XVII. It is a sec-of Dynasties XIII.-XVII. tion that remains in some portions of it as obscure as it is mysterious. It is indeed only respecting its beginning and close that the monuments have anything to say. The so-called "Turin Papyrus," e. g., shows that the Sebekhotep who founded Dynasty XIII. was the immediate successor of the last sovereign of Dynasty XII.; and there are a few other monumental remains which show that he and his successors, for a while at least, ruled over all Egypt. At the other end of the section there are a number of documents [1] that connect Dynasty XVII. with Dynasty XVIII., and which further show that one of the Manetho abbreviators, Africanus, correctly reported Dynasty XVII. as composed of synchronous reigns, — " Thebans and Shepherds," — the Shepherds being the real rulers and the Thebans being vassal princes, one of whom it was, Aahmes, who succeeded in expelling the foreigners and so founded Dynasty XVIII.

The Manetho lists covering this section are in a state of almost irremediable confusion. They continue to accentuate the dynastic divisions, but they yield no names except six of Shepherd kings. They agree for the most part in making Dynasty XIII. " Theban," and Dynasty XIV. " Xoïte ; " but they assign to each an apocryphal number of kings, with an equally apocryphal dynastic period. But they differ so, as respects the remaining Dynasties (XV., XVI., and XVII.), that the work of reconstruction is made a serious task, — some believe impossible. These last three Manetho Dynasties, however, are the " Shepherd " Dynasties. And as neither monuments nor papyri mention a word as to the rise of the Shep-

---

[1] They are the " Sallier Papyrus, No. I.," which establishes the synchronism of the Shepherd King Apepi with a native prince called Rasekenen ; an *inscription* in the tomb of one Aahmes, who served under King Aahmes in the war of liberation, — an inscription covering four reigns ; the "Abbott Papyrus," showing a line of native princes of the name of Rasekenen, and another *tomb-inscription* of a courtier, also called Aahmes, but surnamed Penneb, who lived in the latter part of Aahmes' reign and survived into the reign of Thothmes III. For a full account, see Chabas' " Les Pasteurs," pp. 16–38, and Brugsch's " History," vol. i. p. 239 ; also, Dr. Birch in " Rev. Arch.," 1859.

herds and but little of their fall, it becomes very important to discover, if we can, what Manetho really did say of the Shepherd Era. To be sure, in view of the particularly glaring contradictions of the lists of these three Dynasties, the prospect of reaching any safe conclusions may appear very discouraging. Nevertheless, I believe it possible to gather the original Manetho story, in outline at least, from the very contradictions of the abbreviators, — an outline that can, moreover, be corroborated in several ways.

| Dynasty. | ? MANETHO. | | EUSEBIUS. | AFRICANUS. |
|---|---|---|---|---|
| XII. | THEBAN. (All Egypt.) | | | |
| XIII. | THEBAN. (All Egypt.) | | THEBAN. | THEBAN. |
| XIV. | THEBAN. (Upper Egypt.) | XOÏTE. (Lower Egypt.) | XOÏTE. | XOÏTE. |
| XV. | THEBAN. (Upper Egypt.) | SHEPHERDS. (Lower Egypt.) | THEBAN. | SHEPHERDS. Six names. |
| XVI. | THEBAN. (Ethiopia.) | SHEPHERDS. (All Egypt.) | THEBAN. | "Other SHEPHERDS." |
| XVII. | THEBAN. (Vassals.) (Upper Egypt.) | SHEPHERDS. (Suzerains.) (All Egypt.) | SHEPHERDS. "Phœnicians." Four names. | "Other SHEPHERDS and THEBANS." |
| XVIII. | THEBAN. (All Egypt.) | | | |

A glance at the above plan will make the proposed Manetho reconstruction somewhat clearer. The last two columns present the lists of Eusebius and Africanus (we start with but two of the abbreviators, so as to make the hypothesis less confusing); the double column preceding exhibits the proposed Manetho reconstruction.

Assured that neither Africanus nor Eusebius, whatever their bias, would intentionally misrepresent Manetho, it may be assumed that their contradictions simply reveal misapprehensions of Manetho's dynastic indications, and particularly of his explanatory remarks. It is not likely that the work of Manetho's they quoted from contained any plan or chart of the Dynasties, even if Manetho had one for his personal use; and only those who attempt to describe such facts without such a chart know how difficult it is to present them in a perspicuous way.

We believe that the contradictions of the lists may be harmonized, if we may suppose that in his review of the period Manetho was endeavoring to make clear two features of the curious history, but that it proved difficult, so correlated were the two facts, to put them into language clear enough to prevent misapprehension. The two points it is supposed Manetho emphasized are: (1) that there was a continuous native line, Theban in its inspiration, all the way through the period from Dynasty XII.

to Dynasty XVIII. ; and (2) that though the native
line thus survived, it had a history of varying fortunes, — a history marked by troubles from within
and from without, — a history full of crises, which
he sought to indicate by his dynastic divisions.

To make our meaning clearer, let us suppose that
Manetho's story, in outline at least, was something
like this : —

(1) That during the period of the so-called Dynasty XII. the native Theban line ruled all Egypt,
and, as was really the case, without a challenge
from any quarter.

(2) That during Dynasty XIII. this was also true,
except that the sovereignty, for some reason or
other, passed to another Theban family, the House
of the Sebekhoteps.

(3) That the history of the native line thereafter
was one of disaster.

(4) That, first of all, the sovereignty of Lower
Egypt was wrested from it by the Xoïtes, who
during the so-called Dynasty XIV. confined the
Thebans to Upper Egypt.

(5) That it was while Egypt was thus divided
that the Shepherds came and conquered.

(6) That the Shepherd Era lasted through the
three Dynasties, XV., XVI., and XVII. ; but that
these dynastic divisions were intended by him simply
to mark the three stages of the Shepherd rule, —
viz., the first stage, marked as Dynasty XV., during

which the Shepherds occupied Lower Egypt, having swept the Xoïtes out of the way ; the second stage, marked as Dynasty XVI., during which the Shepherds possessed themselves of Upper Egypt also, the Thebans having in their turn been driven out, and surviving in their Ethiopian Province, which was added to the crown in the time of Dynasty XII. ; and the third stage, marked as Dynasty XVII., during which time the Thebans, allowed to return, were recognized by the Shepherds as vassal princes, themselves accepting the position, doubtless sullenly, but awaiting their opportunity to recover complete independence.

Now, supposing this outline to have been substantially the original Manetho story, it is easy, scanning carefully the lists of the two abbreviators, to understand how each made his mistakes ; for, contradictory as their lists appear, they are really complements to each other. Each reports, though inaccurately and obscurely, a genuine Manetho statement.

Thus, taking Eusebius first, it is evident that he grasped more accurately than Africanus Manetho's statement as to the continuity of the Theban line throughout the period; for he set down in his list as " Theban " even the first two of the Shepherd Dynasties, XV. and XVI. But in the case of the other two dynasties, XIV. and XVII., he was in all likelihood influenced by the explanations Manetho made as to the relations of parties in those Dynasties.

He was probably, for example, led to consider the
" Xoïtes " as the true Dynasty XIV. because of the
emphasis put by Manetho on the shrunken sovereignty of the Thebans, and possibly also on the personal prowess of the Xoïte Pharaohs ; and so he
failed to note that the Theban line still survived in
the Upper country, though with a shorn dominion.

As respects Dynasty XVII., he was probably led
to report it a " Shepherd " Dynasty — in fact, his
only Shepherd Dynasty — because, while undoubtedly
Manetho mentioned the native line as surviving in
that period (for Africanus quotes that), he probably
laid stress yet more on the fact that in that Dynasty
the Thebans were only vassals, and the Shepherds
were the real rulers of Egypt.

Turning next to Africanus' list, it is also easy,
with the reconstructed Manetho story in mind, to
explain its anomalous features. He, like Eusebius,
accurately numbered the dynastic divisions ; but it
is evident that he failed yet more than Eusebius in
grasping their true significance. He indeed completely overlooked the first Manetho point, — viz., the
continuity of the Theban line throughout the Dynasties notwithstanding its troubles. He was more
impressed with its troubles, more influenced by the
emphasis Manetho put on his second point, — the
contestants and the enemies of the Thebans. Like
Eusebius, he made the Xoïtes to be the true Dynasty XIV., and doubtless for the same reasons. The

remaining three Dynasties he understood to be Shepherd Dynasties, his very description of them sounding like a veritable quotation, — " Shepherds," " Other Shepherds," and " Other Shepherds and Thebans," — and because they were in reality the *de facto*, albeit in the view of an Egyptian priest not the *de jure*, Dynasties.

But the reconstructed Manetho story not only helps us to see how Africanus and Eusebius understood, or rather misunderstood, their author, and serves to reconcile their otherwise inexplicable contradictions ; it will be found to be in harmony also with the other Manetho lists. The Josephus lists do not accentuate the dynastic divisions as clearly as those of Africanus and Eusebius, but they really yield the same story. Josephus was more concerned with Manetho's traditions respecting the Shepherds than with the chronology of the era. His object in quoting at all was to identify the Hyksos as the Hebrews. But the very traditions he quotes would show that the Shepherds' stay in Egypt was marked, as the reconstructed story would say, by stages ; that however sudden the initial movement was, the conquest of the country was effected by degrees ; and that there was a marked difference in the attitude of the Shepherds, comparing the earlier and later stages, — that whereas they were at first merciless and despotic, they changed erelong to another mood, and became more tolerant, nay, almost Egyptianized, though the Dynasty was hated none the less, and remained throughout a government of foreigners.

The contradictions of the remaining lists need not detain us, as all of them were really compilations, gathered from the lists of Africanus, Eusebius, and Josephus.

It may be added that the outline we are imagining to have been the original Manetho story is not mere fancy; for not only does it help us, as we have seen, to explain the confusing lists of the abbreviators, it is also in harmony with the very few hints the monuments furnish respecting the earlier and the later order of events. It has already been stated that the monuments certify that the earlier Pharaohs — such of them at least as are assignable to Dynasty XIII. — ruled over all Egypt. This was undoubtedly true as late on as the reign of Sebek-hotep IV.; but there is no hint that succeeding Pharaohs were obeyed so far north as Tanis. Sebek-hotep V., for example, is traced no farther north than Bubastis; from which one may fairly infer an already shrunken dominion. Traces of the subsequent Pharaohs are met only in Upper Egypt, and at length only in Ethiopia.[1]

That Egypt was weakened and divided may be gathered from the exceedingly brief reigns of the Turin Papyrus; for there is scarce one of them that is assigned a longer reign than four years, while

---

[1] Brugsch's History, vol. i. p. 192, also p. 387.

some of them were counted by months, and some even by days, — all of which betokens an era of disputed successions and probably assassinations. As to the Shepherd Era, it has also been stated that the monuments have nothing whatever to say of their coming, but they do have something to say of their going; and the glimpse these important monumental texts give of the condition of things is precisely that of the reconstructed story. They bring to view a native line of princes that seems somehow to have survived; but they are vassals, and the Shepherds are the masters of the land.

Another argument in favor of the hypothesis is what may be styled the continuity of Egypt's history and civilization, notwithstanding its apparent interruption by the Shepherd sway. The Egypt of Dynasty XVIII., as it emerges out of obscurity, though of course in some respects modified by its severe discipline, is the very same in every essential particular as the Egypt of the Usertesens and Sebekhoteps of Dynasties XII. and XIII. Now, one can understand how such a survival would be possible after a period of subjugation, however long, that did not really annihilate the native succession; but it would amount to a miracle if witnessed after even a period of 150 years of a foreign yoke that recognized no native line, to say nothing of the longer period which some would assign to the Shepherd rule.

It is not altogether without reason, then, that we reconstruct the history of this obscurer section of our period on the basis of the reconstructed Manetho lists, and find the key to the problem's solution in the hypothesis of a continuous native line throughout the period, notwithstanding its varied fortunes. The monuments establish the synchronism of the latter part of Dynasty XVII. with the closing years of the Shepherds; and if this is true, why may not it have been equally true of other parts? May not the native line have maintained at least the semblance of continuity all through those dark ages? It is, at any rate, possible in this way to explain what is otherwise inexplicable.

But granted that the outline given of the history of this obscure section of our period may be claimed as more than hypothetical, the inquiry will still remain as to its chronology. It may be asked, Is it possible to even conjecture with any show of reason as to the probable time covered by these Dynasties, XIII. to XVII.? We think it is. Much of course depends on the length that must be assigned to the Shepherd rule. This is prolonged to centuries by some, to be sure, but simply on the basis of the Manetho numbers. These numbers, however, respecting the Shepherd Era particularly, are in inextricable confusion. No two writers that have discussed them agree in their results. It is indeed unsafe to accept any numbers of the Manetho lists without corroborative evidence. On the other hand, there is a possible clew as to the chronology of at least the Shepherd Dynasties, suggested by the very position of the named Shepherd kings in the Manetho lists.

It is true that the lists appear to contradict each other in this, as in so many other respects. For it will be observed that Africanus puts all six of the Shepherds in Dynasty XV.; while Eusebius puts them — at least the four only whom he gives — in Dynasty XVII. But this is probably only another instance of the way in which the two abbreviators understood Manetho's statements. All is easily enough explained if we may suppose that Manetho really intended the six names to cover the entire period of the Shepherd occupation, from its beginning to its end. If, therefore, we may suppose that this is what Manetho meant, then Africanus was right in putting the beginning of the list in Dynasty XV., but erred when he put all six of the list in that Dynasty. The monuments prove that one of them, at any rate, Apepi, belonged to the Seventeenth Dynasty; for he was a contemporary of the Rasekenen with whom began the war of liberation. What Manetho probably said was that the Shepherd rule in its relation to the native line could be distinguished by three stages, important enough to be marked off as Dynasties, and that their government was formally erected in Dynasty XV., under Salatis, the first

Shepherd Pharaoh. He probably added that he was succeeded by the five names that followed, — meaning, not that they all belonged to Dynasty XV., but that the rest of the Shepherd rule was covered by those names.

That Eusebius put the names in Dynasty XVII. followed of course from his conception of that Dynasty as the only Shepherd Dynasty. But it is possible, also, that he would be justified by the facts in putting even Salatis in Dynasty XVII. We are not to imagine that Dynasties XV. and XVI. were long. It is altogether likely that they were brief. The dynastic division was intended to mark not so much the time they occupied as the relative position of the Shepherds and the native line throughout the era. All the traditions suggest that the invasion of Egypt was sudden at the start, and rapid enough in its progress, until the galling yoke was riveted on the whole land. Salatis would be sure to establish his seat at Memphis as soon as possible. Having done that, and so secured his rear, he would be able to advance to the conquest of Upper Egypt. This accomplished, he would not be likely to remain there long, and as a consequence it is not likely that the banished princes would be long kept out of Upper Egypt. What would be more natural than for them very soon to cross the border, and gradually creep down the river, and so inaugurate that period of collisions, of which tradition speaks, which ended in mutual concessions and at last in recognition, — the Shepherds contenting themselves with a suzerainty of the Upper country, and the native line accepting the position of vassals, until the end came. It is not impossible, therefore, that the king who conquered Lower Egypt was the same that conquered Upper Egypt also, and that he even survived into the so-called Dynasty XVII. It may help us to understand why Eusebius made but the one Shepherd Dynasty. He probably gathered from Manetho's statement that the time occupied by Dynasties XV. and XVI. was inconsiderable, and that, though the Shepherds were in the country, the Thebans during those two earlier stages of the occupation did not succumb to Salatis, but kept up the succession, though confined in Dynasty XV. to Upper Egypt, and in Dynasty XVI. to Ethiopia. He also gathered that at length the Thebans found it expedient to acknowledge Salatis, and so inaugurated the third stage, marked as Dynasty XVII., which Eusebius inferred could properly enough be called a Shepherd Dynasty, not only because it was a *de facto* government, as were the other two stages indeed, but because it was acquiesced in by the princes of Egypt themselves and for so long a period. It cannot but be observed how the supposition harmonizes all the facts of the case.

Reasoning in this way, then, it is evident that the major part of the period covered by the six reigns[1] could easily enough be assigned to Dynasty XVII.[2]

If this clew, then, furnished by the very contradictions of the Manetho lists, be accepted, it would suggest that the Shepherd Era may be carried back from the date of the Expulsion scarcely farther than the foundation of the government by the first of the six names Manetho has preserved, the time occupied by the conquest up to the occupation of Memphis being at most but a few years.

[1] Why did Eusebius report but four names? The answer may probably be found in the fact that his last name is "Apepi;" for while six of the Manetho lists give six names, five out of the six make Apepi the fourth king. The inference therefore is not unfair, that there were two, if not three kings between the Apepi who was contemporary with the Rasekenen of the "Sallier Papyrus" and the Shepherd who was Aahmes' contemporary.

It is also probable that, discussing the war of liberation, Manetho stated that it began under Apepi; and he probably referred to Apepi as the last great Shepherd king, — the last whose sway was undisputed, or as the Shepherd in whose reign the resistance began which issued in Egypt's freedom. And Eusebius may have thence inferred that the Dynasty ended with him. The shorter lists probably looked on the commencement, and the longer, the end of the liberation conflict, as the proper closing-point of the Dynasty.

[2] That Eusebius calls the Shepherds "Phœnicians," is doubtless a reminiscence of a genuine Manetho statement, but another instance of misapprehension or of inaccurate reporting. The Shepherds were, it is more than probable, Semitics. The great migration from the world's cradle which modern writers believe issued in the Shepherd Invasion of Egypt, can be best explained, as Dr. Brugsch does, as Semitic in its inspiration. But it can readily be understood how the movement, as it swept along, dragged with it fragments of other peoples found in its path, and sought helpers wherever they could be found. The Phœnicians became very early the world's carriers, so that there would be nothing unlikely in the supposition that they were pressed into the service of the Semitics and helped them by sea and by land. So valuable indeed may have been their assistance, that to many they may have seemed the most important section of the invaders. And Manetho may have so emphasized what the Phœnicians did, that Eusebius was misled thereby as to the ethnic character of the Shepherds themselves.

But this clew does not remain unsupported. It is corroborated, indeed, in a very remarkable way by a monumental time-period of the Shepherd Era, which was discovered a few years ago at Tanis.

It is certainly an interesting circumstance to find any era at all mentioned on the monuments; for this one, if such it be, is the only one known. The Egyptians, as far as known, computed time simply by the regnal periods of their sovereigns, not by eras. It is consequently more curious still that the only instance of an era thus far discovered should have respect to the Shepherds.

It is found on a tablet at present in the Boulak Museum.[1] The tablet is a memorial stone which was originally set up in the sanctuary of the Great Temple at Tanis by an Egyptian courtier, named Seti, at the instance of Rameses II., and as an act of homage on the king's part to his father.

Unfortunately, the inscription does not state the year of Rameses II. when the stone was dedicated. It may have been intended to commemorate his father's death, and so have been set up in the first year of his sole reign; or it may have been set up in his fifth year, — the date of his Asiatic campaign, when, as is known, he was in Tanis, — inasmuch as the tablet refers to a visit of the king to Tanis. There

---

[1] For a full account of the tablet, with Dr. Birch's translation, see "Records of the Past," vol. iv. p. 33 ; also, Chabas in the "Zeitschrift" for 1865 ; also, Mariette's "La Stèle de l'an 400," and De Rougè, "Rev. Arch.," Feb., 1864.

is therefore some uncertainty, amounting however to a few years only, as to that end of the era mentioned on the tablet. The tablet is dated "the fourth day of the month Mesori [i. e., the twelfth month] of the four hundredth year of the king of the Upper and Lower country, *Set-aa-pehti-neb-ti.*" This name is commonly abbreviated to "Set-neb-pehti," or "Set-neb," and the era spoken of as the "Set Era." No wonder that Brugsch says[1] that this "must ever continue to be the most wonderful memorial stone" of the many recovered from the temple-city; for the "Set-neb-pehti," from whose reign the era dates, can be none other than a Shepherd king. This is conceded by all Egyptologists; and as is also agreed upon by most of them, he can only be identified with the "Set Shalt" of another Shepherd monument discovered by Mariette, and he can be none other than "Salatis," the first of the six Manetho Shepherds.[2]

---

[1] History, vol. ii. p. 94.

[2] See Canon Cook in "Speaker's Com.," vol. i. p. 448. There can be no doubt that "Salatis" is a Greek transcription of the original Semitic "Shalt" or "Shalati," the "powerful" or "powerful ruler." It is, of course, to him alone that can be referred the inscription found by Mariette on a Tanis statue, "Set Shalti, beloved of Sutech, lord of Avaris."

Now, as Canon Cook suggests, the "Set-neb-pehti" (i. e., "Set, lord of might" or "powerful lord") of the Tanis tablet was probably the Egyptian translation of the Semitic name which he adopted for his second cartouche, "Set Shalti" being the first cartouche name. While, therefore, all seems conjectural, all is not mere assumption. At any rate, both names mean the same thing, and it is only to the first of the six Shepherd kings that the name of the Tanis tablet can by any possibility be referred. There would be a propriety in the first Shepherd king's adoption of the name "Set," as the era to which it gave a name probably coincided, as Canon Cook says, with the

If the exceptional character of the dating of such a Rameses tablet seems inexplicable, we are to remember that it was set up at Tanis.

Tanis was altogether associated with the Shepherds by the Egyptians. While not really founded as a new town by them, as a famous passage in the Book of Numbers would lead one to surmise, the spot having been occupied by sovereigns of Dynasties XII. and XIII. and possibly before,[1] the Shepherds undoubtedly adopted it as an important strategic point, and so added to or rebuilt it that it became virtually a new city. It was their principal town,[2] and was so identified with them that after they evacuated it, it was dismantled,[3] and from that time and all through Dynasty XVIII. it was entirely ignored by Egypt's sovereigns, and only again became a great city and a royal residence with the rise of Dynasty XIX. It became the favorite capital of Rameses II. It would seem, moreover, that its association with the Shepherds was never quite forgotten; nay, that the inhabitants of the region had preserved the Shepherd traditions. It certainly shows the influence of these traditions, that the sovereigns of the Nineteenth Dynasty should have so honored the Shepherds' God as to give his name a place in a royal cartouche. It

"formal recognition of the god Set as the chief object of worship to the Dynasty." It is in this way that Egyptologists identify "Set neb pehti" as "Salatis," the first king.

[1] Maspero's Histoire, p. 100.  [2] Idem, p. 105.
[3] Idem, p. 171 and p. 206.

was a novelty in Egypt for the son of a native sovereign to be called Seti, so that the succession embraced a Seti I. and a Seti II. and a Prince Seti; and this is the more remarkable because it is known that the naming was exceedingly repugnant to the Theban priests.

The wonder therefore diminishes that, as the chance discovery shows, a prince of the royal family, himself named Seti, commemorating at his sovereign's command the deceased Seti, the king's father, and erecting the memorial at Tanis, should have dated it with the traditional Shepherd Era. Undoubtedly, we may fairly gather from the circumstance that the Shepherd Era yet survived at Tanis and was in popular use there, or at any rate that it could be gathered from the royal registers and with sufficient accuracy to be dated to a month and a day![1]

[1] As an incidental confirmation of the fact that the "Set Era" was known to the Egyptians, and that they looked upon the "Set neb pehti" of the Tanis tablet as the representative Shepherd king, it may be mentioned that when Aahmes, Egypt's liberator, wanted a throne name, he curiously enough took that of "*Ra*-neb-pehti" (Fig. 1). It is as though he retorted to the Shepherds just thrust out, and who looked on "*Set*-neb-pehti" as their great ancestor: "I dethrone your Set and put Ra in his place, and so begin a new era."

Fig. 1.    Fig. 2.

It may be regarded as a further incidental confirmation of the knowledge of the era as still surviving at Tanis, that Rameses I., the founder of Dynasty XIX., who sustained intimate relations with the town, should also have taken for his throne name a simple variation of Aahmes', and adopted it in his cartouche (Fig. 2), "Ra-*men*-pehti." Like

But granted that the dating of the tablet was, as Brugsch regards it, " a survival of a new method of reckoning first introduced by the Hyksos," and granted that the " Set-neb-pehti " was none other than the " Set Shalt " of Mariette's monument and the " Salatis " of the Manetho lists, then it follows that but 400 years elapsed between Salatis and Rameses II.

The initial year of the " Set Era " would of course be the year when Salatis assumed the style of an Egyptian Pharaoh, — a date surely important enough to mark the beginning of an era ; and to fix its precise place, therefore, in the Egyptian chronology becomes a very simple arithmetical problem. It is but needful to subtract from the 400 years the amount of the interval between the Expulsion and the first or the fifth year of Rameses II. to obtain a period of about 150 years for the Shepherd rule, — a period which is not too short nor yet too long for the six named kings.

As to the time that must be allowed for the invasion and conquest, — i. e., up to the establishment of a formal government at Memphis, — it is impossible

Aahmes, Rameses sought to emphasize "Ra" instead of the Shepherds' "Set;" but Aahmes had called him " neb-pehti " ("lord of might"), and so, for distinction's sake, Rameses called him " men-pehti " (" firm " or " established in might "). Such facts will appear more to the point, probably, when it is discovered that these hieroglyphs occur in no other known royal cartouche up to that time, nor afterwards until Dynasty XXIII., which was a " Tanite " House, and so may similarly be construed as a reminiscence of its Shepherd associations.

at present to reach any assured conclusion. It must have been short; for all the traditions make the movement rapid and decisive. It undoubtedly took some time not only to seize the strategic points of the Delta, but to provide for keeping them against surprises. Still, no great length of time was needed for this. Possibly the Numbers passage already alluded to [1] may afford the best time-indication of this interval; for in the mind of the sacred author the one town, Hebron, certainly bore some relation to the other town, Zoan. The passage does not necessarily suggest, as some have inferred from it, that the Shepherds were Hittites; but it probably referred to the fact that the founding of Hebron and the rebuilding of Zoan were the first-fruits of one and the same migration. It is now the fashion to regard the Hyksos invasion as in its inspiration a migration, and, according to Brugsch and most Egyptologists, a Semitic one. But though the wave was, as is likely, a Semitic movement, it seems to have brought in its train tribes of other peoples, particularly Hittites and Phœnicians.[2] It is probable that the pastoral Semitics found it necessary to use the Phœnicians as carriers and the Hittites as builders. It looks as though some of the Hittites stopped in Southern Palestine, and settled where Abraham met them subsequently, — at Hebron, which they founded.

---

[1] Num. xiii. 22.
[2] See note 2 on page 22.

Others of them seem to have gone on with the Semitics; and these it may have been who built, or rather rebuilt, for the Shepherds the " Zoan " of the Numbers passage. So interpreted, the passage would suggest that some seven years elapsed after the Shepherds entered Egypt before they felt it safe to act as though they had come to stay.

At any rate, seven years would be ample, and ten years most probably a long time, to allow for the interval before the formal assumption by Salatis of the style of an Egyptian king.

In this way it is easy to see that the entire Shepherd period, comprising both the conquest and the rule, may not have been more than 160 years.

It may be added, by way of confirmation of the correctness of the conclusions reached, that this " Set Era " of the Tanis tablet can be paralleled by a Hebrew time-period which covers almost the same ground. It will be found possible indeed, before we are through, to harmonize the chronological data both of the monuments and of the Bible, and in so remarkable a way as to justify an appeal to scholars not unnecessarily to extend a possible shorter chronology to a longer one, which is, to say the least, equally hypothetical.

As to the time covered by Dynasties XIII. and XIV., there is no means at present of deciding; for the indications which some would gather from the fragments of the Turin Papyrus are purely hypothetical,[1] and the Manetho numbers are untrustworthy. But happily this question does not directly bear on the special inquiry of these lectures, which is to ascertain the position of the Hebrews in Egypt's history.

It will be enough to discover in the sequel, from a comparison of the Hebrew and Egyptian traditions, that both chronologies substantially agree in making the interval between the birth of Abraham and the Exodus a little more than 500 years ; and so the question as to the time-period of Dynasties XIII. and XIV. may be dismissed for the present, though we are sure that a fair discussion would lead to a far shorter chronology for them than is often claimed.

[1] Aside from the very fragmentary character of this important manuscript, it is not certain how its divisions are to be understood.    Dr. Brugsch (History, vol. i. p. 36) affirms that " its long series of kings was arranged by the author *according to his own ideas and views,*" and that, " as the case stands, no mortal man possesses the means of removing the difficulties which are inseparable from the attempt to restore the original list of kings from the fragments of the Turin Papyrus."

| | II.<br>Josephus. | | III.<br>Africanus. | | IV.<br>Eusebius.<br>(Armen.) | | V.<br>Eusebius.<br>(Canon.) | | VI.<br>Syncellus. | |
|---|---|---|---|---|---|---|---|---|---|---|
| 4 | ARMAÏS | | 4.1 ARMESIS | | 5 | ARMAÏS = DANAOS 5 | ARMAÏS = Dan's 5 | | ARMAÏS = Dan's | 9 |
| | *RAMESSES* | | *1.4 RAMMESES* | *1* | | | | | | |
| | ARMESSES MIAMMON | 66.2 | | | | | | | | |
| | AMENOPHIS | 19.6 | *AMENOPHATH* | *19* | | | | | | |
| 51<br>os) | SETHOSIS = Rameses = Aig's<br>(bro. of Armaïs Dan's) } 59 | | SETHOS | 59 | 51 | RAMESSES = Aig's 68 | EGIPTOS 68 | | RAMESSES =Aig's68 | |
| | | | | | | *AMENOPHIS*　40 | *MENOPHIS*　40 | | | |
| | | | | | | **Dynasty XIX.** | **Dynasty XIX.** | | | |
| | | | | | | *SETHOS*　55 | *SETHOS*　55 | | | |
| 66 | *RAMPSES* | | 66 RAPSACHES | | 61 | RAMPSES | 66 | RAMPSES | 66 | |
| 20 | *AMENOPHIS.* | | AMENEPHTHES | | 20 | AMENEPHTHIS | 8 | AMENOPHIS 40 | AMENOPHIS | 8 |
| 21 | SETHOS = Rameses. | | RAMESSES | 60 | | | | | | |
| | | | AMMENEMNES | | 5 | AMMENEMES | 26 | AMENEMES | 26 | |
| 5 | | | THUORIS | | 7 | THUORIS | 7 | THUORIS | 7 | THUORIS 17 |
| 7 | | | | | | | | | | |

## LECTURE II.

### THE HEBREW CHRONOLOGY.

THE subject of this lecture has been often dealt with as simply a chapter in the Bible's chronology, and without any special reference to its possible bearing on the Egyptian view of the era. But numerous monumental "finds" have made it scarcely possible to study the history of the Hebrews in Egypt as narrated by the sacred writer without comparing it with the statements of the Egyptian scribes. In truth, the interest of the majority of students of ancient Egypt has originated in the Biblical relations of the theme.

Possibly the most diligent student of the era before us has been Lepsius, — a name that Egyptologists pronounce with reverence. His labors have had their reward, in that the student of all time, however he may differ from him, must consult his works. The historical data collected by him are exhaustive and accurate, and will long survive, notwithstanding that his theory has already become obsolete.

It will be impossible to discuss the many questions preliminary to the present inquiry that beset the investigator, — such as, e. g., the question of the value of the Hebrew, as compared with the Greek and other versions of the Old Testament. It may be said, however, that for the purpose of these lectures the Hebrew has been adopted as the standard text, but not to the exclusion of the other versions for reference and comparison. Aside from any prepossession (some may call it prejudice) one may have respecting the authority of the Hebrew Old Testament, the sequel will show that it is as easy, nay easier, to harmonize the Egyptian story, at least of the period under review, with the time-indications of the Hebrew text, as would be the case were any other text adopted as the standard.

It may also be premised that if difficulties were met in attempting to reconstruct the monumental chronology of our period, difficulties equally great will be found in attempting to reconstruct the Old Testament view of it. The Hebrew chronology is, and remains, a stubborn problem. There are, it is true, interpretations of the Scripture time-indications for which plausible arguments may be adduced; but no one of them has as yet commanded universal acceptance, and it looks as though this may be the case for some time to come. It can scarcely be hoped that any revision of the received Hebrew text, now called for, would seriously modify the Pentateuchal time-indications; so that the problem is likely to remain a question of interpretation.

It will be for future monumental "finds" to decide what the sacred writer meant by his time-indications.

The Scripture time-indications that have to do with our period are presented in the two forms of (1) genealogical indications, and (2) a definite time-period.

As to the genealogical indications, there are two features that very soon impress themselves on the investigator : (I) that, according to the Hebrew registers, only a generation or two at most intervened between the death of Joseph and the birth of Moses ; and (2) the jealous care with which the record guards this fact, and disallows its being explained away.

Thus, e. g., the writer not only tells us that Moses was a son of Amram, who was a grandson of Levi, but that his mother Jochebed was "a daughter of Levi," [1] — a statement which, taken literally, would of course ally her to the generation preceding her husband's ; so that one might therefore reasonably infer that by a "daughter" of Levi was simply intended to be understood a female scion of Levi's house. But the narrator forestalls any such inference, and tells us explicitly that we are to understand "a daughter of Levi" as literally such, inasmuch as Jochebed, whom Amram took for wife, was really his aunt, or, as the narrator puts it, "his

[1] Ex. ii. 1.

father's sister ; "¹ so that, as such, she must have been really Levi's daughter.

It follows, therefore, that Moses, on his mother's side at least, was really a grandson of Levi, and consequently that in this way but four generations intervened between him and Abraham. This remains so, moreover, notwithstanding another curious fact which the tables yield, — that in the case of his brother Aaron's wife, Elishaba, who was of the house of Judah, seven generations really intervened between Abraham and herself.²

Such facts certainly show us that the number of generations one may be able to count is no indication by itself of the length of the period covered by them. Generations may be, and are, longer or shorter according to circumstances, and can only be of chronological importance when the genealogical tree gives a basis for calculating the length of the generations. The genealogical indications of the Levitical registers, therefore, while invaluable for corroborative purposes, are not sufficient of themselves to enable us to reconstruct the Bible chronology. A definite time-period is consequently a necessity for this purpose ; and it is given, but unfortunately in such a way as to make it somewhat uncertain how we are to understand it.

(1) The period is first mentioned in the story of

¹ Ex. vi. 20.
² Compare Ex. vi. 33 and Ruth iv. 19.

Abraham (Gen. xv. 13–16).   It is there mentioned as a prediction.

13. And he said unto Abram, Know of a surety that thy seed shall be a stranger in a land that is not their's, and shall serve them ; and they shall afflict them four hundred years ;

14. And also that nation, whom they shall serve, will I judge : and afterward shall they come out with great substance.

15. And thou shalt go to thy fathers in peace ; thou shalt be buried in a good old age.

16. But in the fourth generation they shall come hither again : for the iniquity of the Amorites is not yet full.

God promised Abram that he should have a numerous posterity ; " and he believed in the Lord, and he counted it to him for righteousness."   And it was because of this faith of his that God uttered the special prediction, already recited, respecting Abram and his posterity.

(2) The time-period next occurs in the Exodus story (Ex. xii. 40, 41, 51), where it is not only twice mentioned, but with a special emphasis : —

40. Now the sojourning of the children of Israel, who dwelt in Egypt, was four hundred and thirty years.

41. And it came to pass at the end of the four hundred and thirty years, even the selfsame day it came to pass, that all the hosts of the Lord went out from the land of Egypt.

51. And it came to pass the selfsame day, that the Lord did bring the children of Israel out of the land of Egypt by their armies.

(3) The next time the period is met, is in the New Testament (Acts vii. 6), in a speech of Stephen's, who, while rehearsing before the Council the history of the Hebrew people, naturally referred to God's promise to Abram of a numerous posterity, and therefore quoted the Genesis prediction with its time-period, though he really gives but a summary of the passage : —

6. And God spake on this wise, That his seed should sojourn in a strange land ; and that they should bring them into bondage, and entreat them evil four hundred years.

(4) The last time the period occurs, is in an argument of Saint Paul's (Gal. iii. 17). Paul was maintaining the thesis that "justification is by faith and not by works of the law;" and referring to the fact that Abraham himself was a believer, and that God made the "covenant of promise" with him as such, argued thence, that nothing could ever militate against that irrevocable covenant, and, more particularly, that the law of Moses, subsequently given, could not, nor was it intended to, come between a believer and God : —

17. And this I say, that the covenant, that was confirmed before of God in Christ, the law, which was four hundred and thirty years after, cannot disannul, that it should make the promise of none effect.

Though introduced therefore in this incidental way, the passage itself shows that Saint Paul had in mind both the Genesis prediction and the Exodus fulfilment; and that though he used the number 430, he did not profess to use it with any precision as to details.

Taking the four passages, then, in which the time-period occurs, and bearing in mind their connections, it is easy to see that the problem suggested by them really divides itself into two parts : (1) What is the time-period indicated? and (2) How is it to be measured ?

The difficulty of answering both questions was very early felt. The " Seventy " felt it; for in translating the Exodus passage, they even modified the received text, by making it read (Ex. xii. 40): " Now the sojourning of the children of Israel who dwelt in the land of Egypt *and in the land of Canaan* was four hundred and thirty years." The difficulty has, moreover, survived to the present time. There are those, indeed, who regard the statements and numbers of the four passages as so contradictory as to be worthless. Lepsius, e. g., rejected the number 430. In the dedication of his work on chronology[1] to Baron Bunsen, he explicitly mentions his " entire abandonment of it," though he also deprecates any reflection on the authority of the Old Testament such a course might imply. While thus rejecting the number 430 he puts emphasis on

---

[1] A translation is to be found in Part II. of his "Egypt, Ethiopia, and Sinai," — a volume of Bohn's Antiquarian Library. See pp. 362, 403.

"the Levitical registers of generations, as a far more certain guide," and adds : " If we compare the number of generations in this period, we shall find that there were only four for four centuries." In view, however, of the undoubted genuineness of both the Genesis and Exodus passages, it would seem more philosophical to acknowledge the difficulty, for the moment, of reconciling them, than summarily to pronounce against the authority of both or either of them. And surely any possible interpretation of the passages that would harmonize them may be accepted, though with reserve, and thus relieve one of the need of rejecting them.

Allusion has just been made to the way in which the " Seventy" attempted to solve the problem, — viz., by adding what is really an explanatory clause. To be sure, no addition to the text that would imply it to be a part of Holy Scripture can be defended on critical grounds. It can be looked upon only as a gloss. Nevertheless, it is true that the view of the " Seventy " is in general harmony with Saint Paul's view of the period; for undoubtedly he dates the period from the " covenant of promise," and consequently must have included in it the whole history of Abraham thereafter, as well as the history of the Hebrews, his descendants, up to the time of the erection of the Hebrew commonwealth.

With this general view of the " Seventy " and of Saint Paul it is easy enough to agree, and for a

number of reasons. It is evident, e. g., comparing
the Old Testament forms of the period, that the
time-statement of the prediction was not intended
to be exact, but a general statement sufficiently
accurate for its purpose. The Exodus statement, on
the contrary, professes on its very face to be exact.
The prediction is indeed uttered in two forms that
serve to complete and explain each other.

It is admitted that any one reading the Genesis
passage by itself would be sure to understand its
" four hundred years " to be intended as an exact
period, and to explain its " fourth generation " as
but saying the same thing in another form ; but this
would only be the case as long as it remained a
prediction. When the prediction was fulfilled, and
so the exact time-period known and recorded, as it
is in the Exodus passage, then the most natural
inference respecting the two texts would be that
stated, — viz. that in the earlier text an indefinite
was given for a definite period, and in the later the
statement was intended to be exact. In the Genesis
passage the period is simply counted by generations ;
while in the Exodus passage it is counted not only
by years, but *to a day.*

One can hardly fail to observe what a point the
Exodus narrator makes of his number, not only
twice repeating it, but twice asserting that the four
hundred and thirtieth year was completed on the
very day of the Exodus.

Thus interpreting the Old Testament forms of the period, the New Testament forms of it need occasion but little trouble. Stephen and Paul both had sufficient justification in quoting, the one the Genesis, and the other the Exodus, time-indication. Either number would have been sufficiently accurate for their purposes. Saint Paul, indeed, while adopting the Exodus number, uses it not with precision as to details. It follows, therefore, that the Old Testament 430-year time-period that came to an end on the very day of the Exodus, instead of being discarded, is to be accepted as the veritable measure of time the Bible has given wherewith to thread our way back from the date of the Exodus.

But the second element of the problem then presents itself. Granted that the Old Testament time-period with which we are concerned is the number 430, and granted that it came to an end on the day of the Exodus, the question arises, What is the point of departure for the period ?

The difficulty of satisfactorily answering this question is confessedly great; for undoubtedly a study simply of the two passages containing the prediction and the fulfilment would leave the impression that the time-period is to be dated from Israel's descent to Egypt. But such a conclusion would very soon be challenged by what may be styled another equally Scriptural conclusion. Thus Saint Paul, it is certain, would require us to date it from Abraham's day. Moreover, aside from an Apostle's authority on the subject, — which in this particular instance, other things being equal, one may believe was not intended to be asserted, — there is a very grave difficulty occasioned by the Levitical registers. For if the Exodus passage must be regarded as making *Israel's* sojourn in Egypt to have been 430 years, the registers would deny this, and assert that Jacob and his descendants could not have sojourned in Egypt so long.

These registers indeed create the difficulty in two forms : (1) they show that only four generations, that could cover about 400 years, intervened between Moses and Abraham ; and (2) the specific time-indications of the generations given in the registers themselves make it impossible to adjust these generations to a 430-year period dated from Israel's descent to Egypt.[1]

[1] It is difficult to adjust the time-period, even when dated from Abraham's day, to the few generations between Jacob and Moses. Canon Cook ("Speaker's Commentary," vol. i. p. 301 ), referring to the line through Jochebed, says that "it involves two miracles for which there is no authority in Scripture, — viz., that Levi must have been ninety-five when Jochebed was born, and Jochebed eighty-five when Moses was born." The Canon doubtless exaggerates the difficulty ; for no miracle was required in Jacob's case, who was ninety-one when Joseph was born. At the same time all would admit that such cases are exceptional ; and all must perceive how serious the problem becomes if it is deemed needful to add some two centuries more to the interval. And if some still imagine, as a way out of the difficulty, that some links of the chain in this genealogy, as in others of Holy Scripture, may have been omitted, such a suggestion could hardly be entertained in the present case, in view of the precision with which the sacred writer establishes the exact relationship of all the parties concerned.

These registers at first sight seem to be utterly indifferent about the chronology of the era; but a closer examination shows how curiously the historian does, after all, give sufficient time-data to enable one to form an idea of the lapse of time, — sufficient at least for all needful purposes. Any one who attempts to draw out in a scheme the time-indications referred to will be interested in discovering what checks the Pentateuch furnishes on any attempt unduly to prolong the period. Reference has just been made to the four generations only, e. g., that are enumerated between Abraham and Moses, just as the Genesis passage predicted. But the registers mention a second line from Moses back to Abraham, this time through his father instead of his mother; and, what is an impressive fact to the investigator, in this line the length of each life in the chain is given. The writer tells how Levi lived 137 years; Kohath, his son, 133; and Amram, his son and Moses' father, 137. Taking now these simple elements, the line through Moses' father as well as that through his mother, let any one attempt therefrom to make the family-tree, and he will soon discover the utter impossibility of spreading these generations with their time-indications over a period of 430 years, if it must be dated from Jacob's or Joseph's descent to Egypt.

In this way the Exodus passage would seem to be contradicted not only by Saint Paul, who quotes its number and dates it from Abraham's day, but by the genealogical indications of the Pentateuch. Accordingly, if the Exodus passage must be interpreted as teaching that the 430-year period is to be dated from Israel's descent to Egypt, the difficulty would appear insuperable. It may be added that the difficulty would be yet more emphasized to find that a comparison such as Lepsius has instituted [1] between the genealogical indications already referred to and other co-ordinate indications found in extra-Pentateuchal registers serve only to establish beyond contradiction the brevity of the interval between Jacob and Moses.

There is a necessity, therefore, it must be clear, to revise the interpretation of the Exodus passage so as to bring it into harmony with the genealogical time-indications of the Pentateuch, and likewise with Saint Paul's understanding of the time-period. In some way it must be interpreted, as the " Seventy " believed, to cover a Canaanitish as well as an Egyptian sojourn. And if the question be asked, Is this possible? the reply may at once be made, It is possible. For while without Saint Paul's hint it might not have been discovered, it is yet true that a careful consideration of the two Pentateuch passages will show that not without reason did Saint Paul carry the time-period back to Abraham's day.

The key to the solution may be found, we imagine,

---

[1] Lepsius' Egypt, etc., p. 458.

in the Genesis passage, where the time-period seems to refer to *Abram himself and his seed.* This may be gathered not only from the fact that the " four hundred years" of the thirteenth verse must be the same time-period as that referred to in the sixteenth verse as to come to an end "in the fourth generation," but because God .was evidently dealing with Abraham as the representative of his posterity.

Some may perchance demur at this; but one cannot long dwell on the place of Abraham in the Bible without observing that in all the divine transactions with him God regarded him as a representative believer. He and his seed are contemplated as so completely one that their history is a part of his and his a part of theirs. Moreover, as respects the immediate point before us, can one help observing how wonderfully the history of the Hebrews in Egypt reflected that of Abram? He went down to Egypt, and sojourned there, and was afflicted there, and was sent away too, at the last, after God had plagued Pharaoh's house because of him, and sent away with much substance. Nay more, God seems to lay stress on the fact that the Hebrews in Egypt were to be strangers in a strange land, just as Abram himself at that very moment was a sojourner in a land not yet in possession, — a suggestion that not only completes the parallel, but seems to hint that the period mentioned was intended to cover both sojourns. Is not it possible to paraphrase the

Genesis prediction with this idea in mind, and so make clearer what it was probably intended to include? It may be paraphrased thus: " This covenant I make not with thyself alone. Because of thy faith in my promise of a numerous posterity, I include that seed of thine in this covenant. And to show how true this is, I will foretell something of the days to come. Thou shalt become a great multitude. The history of thy seed shall be a repetition of thine. Thou hast been a stranger in this land since the day thou crossed the River ; so shall thy seed be a stranger in a land not theirs. Even thy history in Egypt shall be repeated in that of thy seed. Thy seed shall be a stranger in that very land. Thou wast afflicted there ; so shall thy seed be. I judged Pharaoh and plagued him because of thee ; so will I judge Egypt because of thy seed. Pharaoh sent thee away ; so will he thrust out thy seed. And as thou wentest out with substance, so also shall it be with thy seed; they shall not go out thence empty-handed. When will all this occur, dost thou ask ? The end will not be in thy day. Thou shalt go to thy fathers in peace; yea, be buried in a good old age. Some four generations of thy seed must intervene before all shall be fulfilled. This history of thee and thine — this history of sojourn in a strange land and of persecution, that has characterized thy life and will be repeated in that of thy seed — will cover some four hundred years ; but at the end of this long period, long after thou hast fallen on sleep, thy seed shall come out of the land of their sojourning, and with great substance. Moreover, by that time the Amorites will be ripe for vengeance. Their iniquity is not now full."

Is such a paraphrase unfair? It may at least be claimed for it that it is in harmony with the headship and representative character of Abraham, — a view that is as much a New as an Old Testament idea. It is, at any rate, a possible interpretation of the Genesis passage. The prediction was suggested by the very nature of the covenant God was at that moment entering into with Abram. The covenant included him and his seed; and the prediction, while forecasting the history of his seed, regards that history as his. The sixteenth verse particularly states that that seed, yet in his loins when the prediction was uttered, should " come hither again;" thus hinting that the time that should elapse was to be dated from Abram's own day.

This interpretation of the prediction is, moreover, not out of harmony with the Exodus passage as it can be interpreted; for it is possible to regard " the children of Israel " of the Exodus passage as simply a parallelism for " the seed of Abraham " of the Genesis prediction. They are called in Exodus " the children of Israel " because that had come to be, as it long continued, the specific designation of the descendants of " Abram the Hebrew." It is to be noted that the Hebrews had in fact two names. It is evident from the Genesis and Exodus story that the Egyptians knew and referred to them as " Hebrews." Among themselves, however, this name, while never entirely disused, came to be used less and less, until that of " the children of Israel " came to be the almost constant designation. At the same time their descent from " the Hebrew " was never forgotten ; so that an apostolic letter even in New Testament times could be addressed " to the Hebrews."

The sacred writer who was recording the exact fulfilment to a day of the prediction uttered by God to Abram evidently regarded " the children of Israel " and " the seed of Abraham " as convertible terms, and, however obscurely some may still think he expressed the thought, no doubt intended the 430-year period to coincide with the 400 years of the prediction. The whole period was a period of sojourn and persecution. The Egyptian sojourn of the seed of Jacob was but the culmination of the sojourn of the Genesis passage, which contemplated the history of Abram and his seed as one. The two passages must be interpreted by the dominating thought of each. In the prediction the thought is of the history to come as the history of Abram's seed, or rather as the history of Abram still, culminating in that of his seed. In the fulfilment emphasis is put on the precise close which the day of the Exodus put on that history, which from begin-

ning to end had been a story of sojourn and persecution. The one passage lays stress on the *representative
position of Abram;* the other, on *the exact fulfilment of
the prediction* made to him as the head of his people.

At any rate, in some such way alone is it possible
to bring the two Pentateuch passages into harmony
with each other, into harmony with the time-indications of the Levitical registers, and into harmony
with Saint Paul's understanding of the era. And if
for any reason the attempt be disallowed, then the
true interpretation will remain an insoluble problem,
and one must not reject the passages, but wait for
further light.

Reasoning then in this way, one may conclude
that the beginning of the time-period of 430 years
is to be looked for in the era of Abraham; and
the only remaining question is as to its intended
initial year.

As to this point it might at first be naturally
enough inferred that the initial year would be the
date of the Genesis prediction, and particularly as
Saint Paul seems to make this his point of departure.
But while Saint Paul evidently believed that the 430-
year period would carry one back to Abraham's day,
he was not indulging in a formal historical review of
the period. He used even the definite number in-
definitely, — i. e., without regard to its exact beginning or end. His argument had to do with Abraham
as the representative believer of all time; and his

strong point was that the covenant God made with
him as such — the covenant of promise — was made
long before the time of the Lawgiver and his law.
The two dates Saint Paul adopts, that of the covenant
of promise and that of the giving of the law, were
near enough to the real dates, and better suited the
form of his argument. It was no part of Saint Paul's
purpose to settle the precise initial year of the period, any more than its precise date of ending.

But there is one insuperable difficulty that would
prevent our adopting the date of " the covenant
of promise" as the initial year of the time-period,
— viz., that it is impossible to fix that date with
precision. It is only known that the prediction was
uttered some time during Abram's first ten years'
sojourn in the land of Canaan, and that it was after
he had been to Egypt and before he took Hagar to
wife.[1] Now, considering the emphatic way in which
the close of the time-period is mentioned as known
*to a day*, it would scarcely be allowable to accept an
approximate date for its beginning. Moreover, if
the view insisted upon of the representative character
of Abraham and his history of sojourn be the true
one, one could scarcely err in accepting as the initial
year of the period that date which the sacred writer
himself gives with precision, — the age of Abram
when he crossed " the River," and so inaugurated
that history of sojourn in a strange land, and of

[1] Compare Gen. xv. 1 and xvi. 3.

persecution withal, which was to culminate in the strangely similar experiences of his seed in the land of Egypt. That was an era of promise also, and an era of faith.[1] In truth, several times during those early years of sojourn did God appear to Abram for his encouragement, though not in so intensely solemn and formal a way as at the time of the Genesis prediction, when God entered into so fast a compact with him that the historian could call it a " covenant." [2]

At any rate, Abram's crossing " the River " seems to have not only given him a name that still survives, but to have furnished a date which the sacred writer deemed most worthy of definite commemoration. It would, therefore, also seem to be the date intended to be the initial year of the period that so intimately concerned Abram and his seed.

We may say, therefore, in concluding this review of the Hebrew chronology of our period, that one may accept from the Pentateuch story with but little hesitation the time-period of 430 years as a definite period, — a period exact to a day as it came to a close, and to be dated from the day which should be the day of days in the calendar of a Jew, — the day when " the Hebrew " crossed " the River," thus separating himself from the past and beginning a history without an ending.

[1] Heb. xi. 9.　　　　[2] Gen. xv. 18.

## LECTURE III.

### JOSEPH IN EGYPT.

IN the chart which has been prepared to facilitate
the work of comparison that is to occupy us in the
remaining lectures, the attempt has been made to
indicate what is certain and what remains uncertain,
— these latter time-factors being represented by the
dotted portions of the lines.

Scanning first the Hebrew part of the chart, it will
at once be observed to what strict limits the Levitical
Registers confine us. At one end of the line it is
but a sum in addition, that, starting with Abram's
seventy-fifth year as the initial year of the Hebrew
time-period, would oblige us to fix the date of Joseph's
death as the year 286 of that period ; and it is a yet
simpler calculation, at the other end of the line, that
fixes the birth of Moses as the year 350 of the period,
— thus leaving a possible interval between the two
events of but sixty-four years. It must further be
observed with what precision the Registers fix the
place, in the Hebrew time-period, of Joseph's fourteen
years of plenty and of famine. It should be emphasized therefore, at the very start, that the dates thus

fixed cannot be debated. If we are justified in adopting from the Pentateuch its 430-year period and in dating it from Abram's seventy-fifth year, then the dates referred to are stubborn factors, that remain fixed points of departure for any possible comparison with the Egyptian chronology.

Scanning next the Egyptian part of the chart, it will be observed that there are, similarly, fixed as well as uncertain time-factors. We refer now not only to the regnal periods that are certain, but to the "Set Era" of the Tanis tablet, which in so curious a way forms an almost exact parallel with the Hebrew time-period itself. For if we are justified in adopting it at all, it certainly carries us back 400 years, from some year of Rameses II. to the beginning of the Shepherd dominion. And it cannot but be observed how, within specific limits, this era remains a fixed element, whichever Egyptian chronology we adopt, furnishing an important corroborative standard with which to compare parts of the period that are uncertain, and forbidding undue estimates of intervals.

The chart presents five possible Egyptian Registers for comparison with the Hebrew time-period, representing the differing opinions of Egyptologists on the chronology of our period. A comparison of these five Registers will reveal a much less degree of divergence of opinion among Egyptologists respecting this period than may have been imagined.

All the Registers, for example, present the same chronology for the period between the accession of Aahmes and the death of Amenophis IV., — a period of about 198 years. And they further agree as to the regnal periods of Seti I. and Rameses II., assigning to the latter Pharaoh his monumental sixty-seven years [1] and to Seti I. the thirty years, for which there seems good reason.[2]

[1] In the "Academy" of July 3, 1886, may be found the "Procès verbal," by M. Maspero, of the unwrapping of the mummy of Rameses II., which, with many other royal mummies, came from the Deir-el-Bahari "find." According to Maspero, the Rameses face bears rather an animal expression than of high intelligence, coupled, however, with a certain decision of character and an air of kingly majesty. The body is that of "an old man, but vigorous and robust." He adds : "It is known that the sole reign of Rameses II. was sixty-seven years, and that he must have died almost a centenarian."

[2] In the "Academy" of July 31, 1886, may be found a similarly precise account, by Maspero, of the unwrapping of the mummy of Seti I., found also at Deir-el-Bahari. We are told that "the condition of the body would suggest that the sixtieth year had been long passed, confirming the opinion of savants that attributes to him a very long reign." But though old, it is not necessary to infer thence that he began to reign very early. There are indications that look the other way. It has been suggested as very probable, that his father and Horus (of Dynasty XVII.) were brothers, and both therefore contemporaries of Amenophis IV.; for Horus was his general. If this be so, it is then likely that Seti was no longer young when his father died. That he should associate his son with him on the throne at so early an age would certainly suggest some reason for such haste, — a reason that might well enough have been his own advancing years. The monuments yield only his twenty-fifth year; and it is certainly sufficient, therefore, to put his regnal period at thirty years. This would allow some eighteen years of an associated reign with his son, and that much of an associated reign for Rameses II. would seem to be required by the story of Rameses' wars. As an instance of the mistakes sometimes made by the most exact of men, allusion may be made to the fact that Maspero ("History," p. 218) should say that Rameses II. "made war in Syria from the time he was ten years old;" whereas, putting together all the data, he could not well have been less than thirty (he was probably at least thirty-three) at the time of his Syrian war; for as the story of that war of his fifth year shows, he was old enough to have sons in command of army corps. No wonder that Brugsch ("History," vol. ii. p. 67) found it difficult to refrain from

THOTHMES III.

The five Registers differ indeed as to three points only: (1) As to the interval between the death of Amenophis IV. and the accession of Seti I. This interval is differently treated by different writers; the divergence in this case, however, amounting to but twenty years. (2) As to the length of Mineptah's sole reign; some making this eight, and others twenty years.[1] (3) As to the Exodus era; three of the Registers synchronizing this with the close of Mineptah's reign, and the other two synchronizing it with the close of Dynasty XIX. But the total divergence of the five Registers amounts to less than fifty years.

Advancing now to a comparison of the five possible Egyptian chronologies with the Hebrew time-period, some interesting conclusions will be reached at once.

It will be observed, e. g., that the chronology of three of the Registers (I., III., and IV.) would oblige us to place Joseph's fourteen-year period in the reign of Thothmes III., while that of Register II. would synchronize it with the reign of Amenophis III. On the other hand, the chronology of Register V. would

chaffing the savant, saying: "The presence of these grown up sons will prove to a French scholar that Rameses II. could not have fought at Kadesh as *a boy of ten years.*" No doubt Brugsch makes the sons too well-grown; but the fact is certified to by the inscriptions, that he had sons with him who were at least in formal command of named divisions.

[1] The monuments yield but his eighth year, which was probably its limit. The twenty years assigned by some is based on the Manetho numbers, which, as usual, vary in the lists; some making the regnal period eight, others twenty. It must be evident that the latter number is simply the addition of the twelve associated years and his eight sole years.

oblige us to divide the period among three different Pharaohs.

We may therefore at once reject Register V.; for the Scripture story undeniably leaves the impression that the period in question belonged to a single reign.

Examining next the three Thothmes' Registers (I., III., IV.), it will be observed that they would oblige us to date Joseph's elevation, respectively, in the fortieth, thirty-eighth, and twenty-sixth years of that Pharaoh.

Now, we may at once dismiss Register IV., because it is a monumental fact that the whole reign of Thothmes III. up to his fortieth year was a constant succession of foreign wars, and the chronology of Register IV. would oblige us to synchronize some of his most brilliant foreign campaigns with the seven years of famine, — a conclusion that one could hardly accept.

We may also dismiss Register III., that puts the elevation of Joseph in the thirty-eighth year of Thothmes; for while, did necessity compel, it might be accepted, inasmuch as it would merely oblige us to consider that Thothmes continued his campaigns during the first two of the plenteous years, Register I. is to be preferred, — for not only does it perfectly adapt itself to the two stories of Joseph and Thothmes, but, what is of more importance, the chronology of the Register as a whole is more trustworthy than that of Register III.

Consequently, only the two Registers (I. and II.) will remain for the work of comparison.

Scanning these two Registers, then, it will be observed that while they both include in their reckoning the three brief reigns with which Dynasty XIX. closed, Register I., throughout the debatable portions of the era, adopts.the shorter, while Register II. adopts the longer chronology, — the difference in time between the two, however, amounting to but thirty years in all.

Accordingly, if we adopt the longer chronology, Joseph's fourteen-year period must be assigned to the reign of Amenophis III.; whereas, if we adopt the shorter chronology, Joseph's period must be carried back to the reign of Thothmes III.

The question may be asked, Which one of these two Pharaohs is the more likely to have been the Pharaoh of Joseph's elevation?

In reply, it may be said at once, that were we at liberty to accept at will either of the two chronologies as equally trustworthy, it would be difficult to decide which of the two Pharaohs would better answer to the requirements of the Hebrew story. The monuments show that the wars of Thothmes III. were virtually over after his fortieth year, and that he had the fourteen additional years needed yet to live; and the wars of Amenophis III. were all over before at least the plenteous years had passed by, if we adopt that chronology, with abundance of regnal years yet remaining to more than cover the fourteen-year period.

Both of them, moreover, were great Pharaohs; for if Thothmes III. was, as some think, the greatest of Egyptian kings, Amenophis III. was not far behind him. As a builder, indeed, he was quite as famous as his prototype. It would therefore be really difficult to decide between them, whether as respects the events of their reigns or their place in Egypt's history.

Some may, however, imagine that the era of Amenophis is to be preferred, because, if the chronology of that Register is adopted, it would allow the death of Jacob to fall in the same reign as the fourteen-year period; whereas that of Register I. would assign the event to a date some twelve years after the death of Thothmes III. But there is something to be said in favor of the chronology of Register I. on this very ground; for the Genesis story of Jacob's death and burial seems to imply that by that time some change had occurred, affecting Joseph's position in Egypt. The Genesis passage (Gen. l. 4, 5), tells how, after the days of mourning had ended, Joseph did not himself ask Pharaoh's permission to bury his father in the land of Canaan, but " spake unto the *house of Pharaoh*," and sought their intercession with Pharaoh on his behalf, saying, " If now I have found grace in your eyes, speak, I pray you, in the ears of Pharaoh, saying," etc. To be sure, this may be otherwise explained. Still, the state of things naturally suggested by the words would be in complete harmony with the chronology of Register I. We are not at liberty to suppose that Joseph maintained the position to which his Pharaoh exalted him throughout his remaining career, for he lived eighty years after his elevation. A change came, it is likely, with the first new reign ; though Joseph was doubtless respected, and continued to be almost as influential with succeeding kings as long as he lived.[1] It may be, therefore, that the passage in Genesis is really to be explained as a hint of a new reign intervening. At any rate, the fact of Jacob's death occurring in a subsequent reign, as Register I. would indicate, is rather an argument in favor of, than against, its chronology.

But there is a further consideration, apart from the conviction that the chronology of Register I. is the more trustworthy, that leads us to make the choice between the two Pharaohs in favor of Thothmes III. as the more probable Pharaoh of Joseph's elevation. We refer to the probable influence of Joseph on the curious history of the reigns succeeding that of Thothmes III.

---

[1] The Talmud mentions a tradition that Pharaoh, Joseph's friend, died long before Joseph died, and that he commanded the son who succeeded him to obey Joseph in all things, and left the same instructions in writing. It also states : "This pleased the people of Egypt ; for they loved Joseph and trusted implicitly in him" See Polano's translation of "The Talmud," one of the "Chandos Classics," p. 118.

If we may trust the chronology of Register I., Joseph survived Thothmes III. some sixty-six years, — a period that entirely covered four of the succeeding reigns; viz., those of Amenophis II., Thothmes IV., Amenophis III., and Amenophis IV. Moreover, the Scripture story would certainly suggest that Joseph was not only not neglected as long as he lived, but was influential enough to protect the rights of his people. The question may therefore be fairly enough put, Is there anything in the further monumental history of the Dynasty that may be explained on the hypothesis of Joseph's presence and influence? We think there is. We refer to the rise and progress of that remarkable religious revolution that culminated, in the reign of Amenophis IV., in the establishment of a quasi-monotheism as the religion of the State.

It was Lenormant who suggested that " the form of religion established by Amenophis IV. stood in a close relation to that professed at the time by the Israelite portion of his subjects."[1] Lenormant saw in the very name of the god so exclusively honored by Amenophis IV., " Aten," a reference to the Semitic "Adonai," and asked the question and answered it: " Had the Hebrews part in this foreign and very imperfect attempt at monotheism? I believe one right in supposing this." He even finds some anal-

---

[1] Manuel d'histoire (Paris, 1868), vol. i. p. 252. Rawlinson's History of Egypt, vol. ii. p. 273.

ogies between the cult of the Hebrews, as finally established by Moses, and that shown on the monu.· ments of Amenophis IV., — e. g., the table of shew-bread and, we may add, the burning of incense.[1]

Dümichen also has pointed out the resemblance between the god "Aten" and the Semitic "Adon" (Lord), observing that "the hieroglyphic group was certainly used with reference to this Semitic name of God."[2]

But whether these things be accepted or not, the fact remains that scions of this Dynasty were more or less alienated from the prevailing creed of the nation, and in one instance completely broke faith with the past, and went so far as not only to discard the Theban god and his worship, but to erect a new capital, with its temple restricted to a single cult, the worship of "Aten."

The revolution did not originate with Amenophis IV. It had been long brewing. It is known that his father, Amenophis III., sympathized with the "Aten" worship, though he did not go to such a length as his son, and completely break with the Theban priests. The revolution can be traced back farther still, — at least to the preceding reign, that of Thothmes IV. In that reign, however, it was scarcely more than a revival of interest in the most ancient

---

[1] See Prisse d'Avenne's "Monuments Égyptiens," Pl. XII., where Amenophis IV. is represented as burning incense to "Aten."

[2] Die Flotte einer Aegyptischen Koenigin (Leipzig, 1868). See particularly his explanation of Tab. III., p. 18.

and purest worship of Egypt, that of the sun. But if it is true that the new school of thought took its rise before the reign of Amenophis III., and we are right in supposing that the religious revival was due in any degree to Joseph's inspiration, then we must of course look for Joseph's Pharaoh before Amenophis III. It is on this account, therefore, that Thothmes III., the Pharaoh indicated by Register I., is to be preferred as the Pharaoh of Joseph's elevation.

But let us look a little more closely at this religious movement, and at Joseph's connection therewith.

What the very earliest worship of Egypt was, it is perhaps impossible to say. But those who have studied the subject most carefully, have noticed that the nearer we get to the beginning of things the simpler and purer dogma becomes. And there are those who affirm that the earliest theology of the Egyptians was monotheistic.[1] The polytheism of which the sacred books became so full can be best explained as the result of an attempt very early made to *describe* the One God, who, according to an expression that often occurs, "manifests himself in millions of forms." If there was any universal worship in Egypt,

---

[1] Brugsch's "Religion und Mythologie" (Leipzig, 1884; only the first half is as yet published). Renouf's "Hibbert Lectures" for 1879. "Rev. Arch.," vol. for 1860, Part I., containing articles by De Rougé on the "Funeral Ritual of the Ancient Egyptians." Pierret's "Essai sur la Mythologie Égyptienne" (Paris, 1879). Lepsius' "Aelteste Texte des Todtenbuchs"; Max Müller on "Solar Myths," in the "Nineteenth Century" (Dec., 1885). Maspero's "Histoire Ancienne" (1886), p. 25 et seq.; also, his "Guide au Musée de Boulaq" (1884), p. 147, on the "Panthéon Égyptien," etc.

it was the sun-worship, founded on the sun-myth.[1] That myth in its origin was intended to be a simple description of phenomena. It took account of the sun in its various positions above and below the horizon, and noted its influence on matter and on life. Afterwards, perceiving the analogies that are so evident between the sun's history and that of a human life, it became philosophical, and sought thereby to explain the origin and history and destiny of all things.

No one would be so bold as to affirm that any Egyptian, at least in the ancient days, accepted the story of Osiris and Isis as veritable history. It was, in the first instance, symbolism, pure and simple. And possibly no more appropriate and adequate a symbol of the Divine Being can be found in Nature, than the sun. No wonder the sun-myth originated so early, and no wonder it stayed so long. At any rate, the sun-worship is the only universal worship met in the most ancient Egypt; and though one or another of the separate sun-gods of the myth came to be prominently emphasized in certain centres, — as Ra at Heliopolis, Osiris at Abydos, and Tum at Memphis, — yet the unity of the myth was never lost sight of.

But the Egyptians did not stop in their philosophizing with the sun-myth. Solar myths form but a part of mythology. All phenomena in the realm of

[1] Maspero's Histoire, p. 211.

Nature and life were thus described and similarly traced to their causes. And how natural it was for them, while dealing with the causes of the phenomena met with in Nature, to find themselves wrestling with the problem of the One Great Cause of all things! It is easy enough to see that the other so-called deities of Egypt — i. e., those not distinctively sun-gods — were originally but expressions for conceptions, more or less philosophical, of the origin of things. The view serves to explain the multitude of local deities, all expressing the same conception. For it is certainly true that in the earliest Egypt no one of these had the pre-eminence. These local deities simply show what philosophical conceptions of the Supreme Being and his attributes were most potent in their localities. Thus, e. g., the Memphis priests, explaining the origin of things, believed that they were made by some Creator; and they called him "Ptah," "the maker or shaper," looking on him as the Demiurge of the universe. The Theban priests put more emphasis on the inscrutable and mysterious character of the Being who was the author of all being, and so called him "Amen,"—"the concealed." But in the beginning these were perfectly co-ordinate conceptions and co-ordinate deities; recognized as such, wherever known. And yet, underlying them all was the idea, that never entirely lost its power, of the One God, who simply "manifests" himself in these almost numberless forms; meaning

thereby to express the variety of his attributes.[1]
While, however, these local conceptions gave rise in
this way to many local polytheisms, the sun-myth
never lost its influence. The Heliopolite priests,
through all changes of Dynasties and of dogmas,
persisted in emphasizing the story of Osiris or Ra,
who was really Egypt's one God. The pious Egyptian, no matter where he lived, was most anxious
at death to be identified with Osiris, and to enjoy
that eternal life which could alone be possessed by
becoming one with him.[2]

Now, while all this was true, circumstances were
ever bringing some one of the local cults into promi-
nence. The establishment of the capital at Memphis, e. g., would be sure to make its god "Ptah"
more important throughout the realm. So, when
Thebes was elevated from the rank of a mere provin-
cial town[3] to become the capital, it was natural that
its local god, " Amen," should then come to the fore.
Moreover, when we remember the place Thebes
occupied in Egypt's history, it is not to be wondered at that its priests, who were so devoted
to Amen, should assert and maintain his pre-eminence. At first, to be sure, these claims were not
put forth to the exclusion of Ptah or of the solar
gods ; but in time Amen was so far pushed to the

---

[1] Hibbert Lectures (1879), pp. 89, 215; also, De Rougé, in "Rev. Arch.,"
1860, p. 230, on "The Seventeenth Chapter of the Ritual."

[2] Hibbert Lectures, p. 184.

[3] Maspero's Histoire, p. 206.

front as to dim the lustre of the other deities, and
at length to claim the place of Ra and to be called
" Amen-Ra."

It is not difficult, also, to understand what jealousies such pretensions would excite among the parti-
sans of the other cults, nor to understand how the
Pharaohs, aware of what could happen should the
Theban priests grow too strong,[1] would do all in their
power to curb the development of the Amen-cult;
only, however, to discover that it was a power behind the throne that they must recognize and even
favor.

Whether Amenophis II. did aught to resist the
growing tyranny, is not known.  His reign was short,
and not much is known of him.  But his successor,
Thothmes IV., whose reign was also brief, seems to
have tried at least to resist the encroachments of
the Amen priests ; for under the pretext of a dream
and of a special Divine command, he cleared away
the sand that was fast burying the old Sphinx, and,
connecting it once more with the ancient worship of
which it was a relic, emphasized the worship of the
sun-god " Hormakhis," — i.e., Horus, or the sun, of the
two horizons.  But for some reason he did not long
survive, and his end is obscure.  But it is evident, notwithstanding the meagre account we have of the details of the movement, that there was in that reign a
marked revival of interest in the purer worship of

---

[1] It did happen at the close of Dynasty XX.

the sun, — a revival that may not altogether be explained from its political side, but could be adequately explained on the supposition of the presence and influence of Joseph. The monuments yield much information respecting the subsequent reign, — that of Amenophis III., who, next to Thothmes III., probably made the profouudest impression on Egyptian history. He was a remarkable Pharaoh, as respects both his public and private history. The one fact of his life, however, that most stirred the Egyptians was that this great Pharaoh should take to wife, not a scion of the royal house, nor even an Egyptian, but a foreigner, — a foreigner, as is now agreed to by Egyptologists, of Semitic blood. Canon Cook emphasizes, as he expresses it, "the strongly marked Semitic features, not to say Jewish, of the mother of Amenophis IV., as gathered from the portraits found on the monuments."[1] Why the great Amenophis thus departed from the traditions of Egypt, no one can affirm; but the sequel, that tells of her influence on him and on her son, shows what an epoch it created in Egypt's history.

Doubtless Amenophis was influenced in what he did, partly at least, by the politico-religious considerations already mentioned; but his marriage undoubtedly strengthened whatever purpose he had formed

---

[1] Speaker's Commentary, vol. i. p. 460. For her portrait see Lepsius' "Denkmaeler," vol. vii. abt. iii.; also, Prisse d'Avenne's "Monuments," Pl. XII.

of resistance to the Amen-encroachments. State-
craft led him still to maintain relations with the
Theban priests, and outwardly he showed them favor;
but he also showed marked favor to the ancient sun-
worship of Heliopolis, and at length, according to
some, established, though not to the exclusion of the
Amen-worship, the special sun-cult, which received its
fullest development under his son's reign. Even those
twin colossi, erected in his reign, that are so conspic-
uous a feature of the Theban plain, completely dominating the horizon in the South as the Sphinx does
in the North, can only be explained as identifying
the king with the sun-god Horus, of the two horizons. At any rate, Amenophis III. celebrated a
festival, which a scarabæus connects with his eleventh
year, of a boat of the solar disc, called " Aten-nefru,"
— i. e., " the most lovely Aten." He was doubtless,
therefore, inclined to the new dogma, but, as Dr.
Birch says, deemed it needful " to introduce it by
degrees." [1]

The son, Amenophis IV., on reaching the throne,
at once openly revolted against the Amen-ascend-
ency ; and that no one might misunderstand his
purpose, worshipped the sun exclusively, regarding
the visible sun, that is so important to the life of the
earth, as symbolical of the invisible God who is the
source of all blessing. He even founded a new capital, and made it the centre of his new cult ; and was

---

[1] Birch's History of Egypt, p. 108.

so much in earnest that he changed his name from
Amenophis to " Khuenaten," as though he would not
even be called by Amen's name. He had also the
courage of his convictions, and felt strong enough to
build an " Aten " sanctuary in Thebes itself, over
against the Karnak temple ; though it was afterwards destroyed, and its materials appropriated.

Now if, as the chronology of Register I. would indicate, Joseph was exalted in the last quarter of the
reign of Thothmes III. and continued to live through
all these succeeding reigns, may we not find the key
to the evidently increasing influence of the creed and
ritual of Heliopolis in his connection therewith ?

It is at any rate true, according to the Scripture
story, that Joseph became connected with Heliopolis,
the old-time home of sun-worship, and even married
into its priestly house, — a fact as startling from the
Egyptian as from the Hebrew point of view. Moreover, the Hebrews, his kindred, seem to have re-
tained a recollection of the Heliopolite ritual, and
of that alone, amid the Divine discipline that en-
deavored to instil into their hearts, as into their creed,
the faith of Jehovah and his spiritual worship.

In the sun-god ritual at Heliopolis the sun-bull of
Osiris (the white bull Mnevis [1] 𓃒 ) played an important part. It was the bull which was colored in
gold when painted on inscriptions; and when cast,
was made in gold or brass.

---

[1] Lepsius' Egypt, Ethiopia, etc., p. 413.

In Egyptian symbolism, while the gods were sometimes represented as men with characteristic emblems,
they were also represented by animals.[1] Amen, e. g.,
was symbolized by a well-grown goose, Ptah by a
beetle, Thoth sometimes by an ibis and sometimes by
a dog-headed ape, Anubis by a jackal. So it was
with the sun-gods. Horus' symbol was the hawk.
A bird (the " Phœnix ") represented Osiris. Ra was
symbolized by a bull. Both the Osiris-Phœnix and
the Ra-bull, " Mnevis," had a home at Heliopolis.
Now, all this was doubtless in the first instance the
purest symbolism, though it degenerated, as it was
sure to do, into a disgusting animal-worship.

The most celebrated of the sacred animals were
the bulls, called by different names at various local
centres, but all pointing to the same god. The
" Mnevis-bull " at Heliopolis was called " the soul of
Ra." The " Apis " bull at Memphis was called " the
incarnation of Osiris." At first this latter was a
pure sun-god ; but at length it was developed into a
complex deity, and was said to have proceeded from
both Ptah and Osiris, and was called " The second
life of Ptah and soul of Osiris." It was " without
father," — its generation was of heavenly origin, " a
ray of light from the sky fertilizing its mother."
The deceased Apis bull became an Osiris, and took
the name of " Osiris-Apis," of which the Greeks
made " Serapis." The bull-worship at Memphis,

[1] Maspero's Histoire, p. 28.

therefore, was not strictly the pure sun-worship. It came to be mixed up with the Ptah worship, just as at Thebes the later worship of "Amen" was developed, as stated already, into the mongrel conception of "Amen-Ra."

The sun-worship was best maintained in its purity at Heliopolis, where all the sun-gods comprised in the sun-myth had their recognition, and the doctrine of the Divine Unity was clearly enough taught in its theological school. This idea was represented by the white bull Mnevis, whose worship, symbolizing as it did "the soul of Ra," kept before the mind of the worshipper the thought that there was after all but one God.

Is it a mere coincidence, then, when the Hebrews lost heart amid the perplexities of the wilderness, that they should have returned, as by an instinct, to a worship with which they had probably been only too familiar?

We all know how, amid the uncertainties of their new life that led them to think themselves deserted of Moses and Moses' God, they set up the golden bull and worshipped it, doubtless as they had done many a time before in Egypt. For, as Lenormant says, there is no doubt but that "during their sojourn in Egypt the monotheism of the Hebrews had become somewhat materialized."[1] Such facts serve to give a greater point to the command writ-

[1] Manuel, vol. i. p. 254.

ten by God's own finger, that, while enumerating
the very forms of worship with which they were familiar, forbade symbolic worship of any description,
and put the command in the Decalogue, as a moral
prohibition of universal obligation. A purely spiritual worship is the most difficult of all achievements,
and apostasy therefrom natural and easy. The tendency is operative still in the symbolism of our own
day, which, innocent as it is claimed to be in itself
and as an aid to devotion, is as important a step
toward idolatry to-day as ever. Nevertheless, it cannot be doubted that Joseph to a certain extent conformed in Heliopolis to its sun-worship. He could
not have married into its priestly house without becoming at least formally associated with its school
and without showing some sympathy with its teaching. To be sure, some may think it a reflection on
Joseph that he should, if he did, even appear to abet
for so many years a style of worship that from the
Scripture's standpoint seems indefensible. But we
are to remember that the Second Commandment
had not yet been given. Besides, Joseph probably
regarded it as simply symbolism. One can understand how Joseph, though retaining to the full his
Hebrew faith, might have seen in the sun-worship
of Heliopolis not only the purest of Egypt's creeds,
but a symbolic way of expressing his own belief that
there is but One God, the source of all life and blessing. Moreover, he may have regarded it as a choice

between evils. He may have reasoned that it was not only easier but wiser to supplant Egypt's polytheism by emphasizing one of its purest dogmas, which could be easily explained as teaching monotheism. If he could not at once overthrow the gods of Egypt, he could try to mitigate the horrors and indecencies of the idolatrous mysteries, by drawing attention to a purer and more beneficent worship which their own priests could teach, and which had been sung from ancient times in many beautiful hymns. He doubtless found a possible ground for sympathy with the Heliopolite dogma, in the original symbolism of the sun-worship, that representing Ra, as it did, both as a man and a bull, did so simply to symbolize on the one hand the intelligence, and on the other hand the creative and upholding strength, of the one God, who is the Author and the Sustainer of the universe of matter and of mind.

From such a point of view it is easy enough to explain the rise and progress of the religious revolution that characterized the middle history of Dynasty XVIII. It throws light on that curious marriage of the third Amenophis, that undoubtedly can be adequately explained by the presence of some of Joseph's kindred in the court circle. It certainly points to the inspiration of her conceded influence on the king respecting the new cult, that was yet so old. It would also point to Joseph's influence on the son, — an influence great enough by that time to

lead Amenophis virtually to abandon Heliopolis itself
as well as Thebes, and establish a new centre for
a yet purer form of the sun-worship. Around the
old centre had doubtless grown up corruptions and
abuses, which Joseph found it impossible to reform
or control. The only thing to be done was, if possible, to induce the king to break with it altogether,
and to establish a virtually exclusive creed and
worship, — " Atenism," recognizing but one god
"Aten," the very name suggesting the Semitic notion
of " Lord " of all. The change of the king's own
name to " Khuenaten " — i. e., " the glory of Aten,"
or " the glory of God " — would certainly show his
own warm sympathy with the new theology.

It is from considerations such as these, that we are
led, therefore, to prefer the era of Thothmes III. for
the date of Joseph's elevation; inasmuch as the
heresy (as some regarded it) certainly took its rise,
though with feeble beginnings, before the time of
Amenophis III., and the heresy itself can be best
explained in connection with the presence and influence of Joseph. Besides, as already seen, it is the conclusion to which the chronology of Register I., that
is more trustworthy than the other, would lead.

But whether in the end it will appear that
Thothmes III. or Amenophis III. was the Pharaoh
of Joseph's elevation, it can be said, at present, that
either of them would abundantly satisfy the conditions suggested by the Hebrew narrative.

AMENOPHIS III.

(1) Each of them had a reign long enough and of a character to answer the requirements of the story of Joseph.

(2) Both were native sovereigns; and cousequently all the arguments that point to a native rather than to a foreign prince, like one of the Shepherds, would equally well apply.

No one with an unprejudiced mind, reading the Hebrew story, would for a moment think of Joseph's Pharaoh as a Shepherd king. There are a number of incidental hints, scattered throughout the narrative, which, brought together, find their most natural interpretation in an Egyptian Pharaoh. Take as an example that "aside," if we may so call it, in Gen. xlvi. 34, which Joseph knew so well how to turn to the advantage of his brethren, — "for every shepherd is an abomination to the Egyptians." To be sure, there are those who, believing Joseph's Pharaoh to have been a Shepherd king, and perceiving the point of the "aside," have tried to explain it to suit their view; but all must feel how forced are their explanations. A Shepherd king would surely not be suggested to the ordinary reader. All, however, is natural enough, if the Pharaoh were a native sovereign, and particularly if of a Dynasty whose founder had expelled the hated foreigners, and who continued to hold in abhorrence the very occupation that would call to mind the Shepherd kings.

Mention may also be made of two important facts
touched upon in the Hebrew story, — viz., Joseph's
connection by marriage with the priestly house of
Heliopolis *at Pharaoh's instance,* and the hints given
in several connections [1] that Joseph's Pharaoh was
king over all Egypt from one end of it to the other.
As to the former point, is it more likely that such a
connection would have been sought for Joseph, or if
sought granted, under a native or a foreign rule?
As to the latter point, it is not certain that such
a universal sway was true of any Shepherd king.
The Delta was doubtless in the complete possession
of some of them for a time, but it is not likely that
their sway over Upper Egypt ever amounted to
much more than a suzerainty.[2] Certainly none of
the Shepherd kings ever so ruled the whole land
as to be able to introduce such important and far-
reaching fiscal arrangements as is asserted in Scripture of the Pharaoh of Joseph.

It may be further stated, that even if a reconstructed chronology would allow the era of Joseph
to be synchronized with the Shepherd Era, there
would be an inexplicable difficulty to remove, occasioned by the continued presence of the Hebrews in
Egypt subsequent to the Shepherds' expulsion. The
question might in such a case fairly enough be

---

[1] Gen. xli. 45, 46 ; xlvii. 20, 21.

[2] Maspero, in his " Histoire," p. 167, says " their sway was scarcely beyond
the Fayoum."

asked, Why were not the Hebrews also expelled from the Delta along with their Semitic neighbors ? Why, in view of the hatreds begotten by the very occupation of the Hyksos, — a hatred that only intensified as time passed by, so that the very sight of one was enough to evoke it anew, — were the Hebrew shepherds allowed to stay ?

On the hypothesis of Register I., which brings Joseph to Egypt long after the Shepherd expulsion, all is explicable. It can be readily understood how in the time of Thothmes III. a simple Hebrew should, for distinguished services to the State, be raised to honor, just as Daniel and Mordecai were rewarded long after in the farther East. It is clear, too, how his evident spirit of loyalty to Pharaoh's interests, coupled with his unfeigned piety, would check any undue jealousy or suspicion of the foreigner. The hypothesis best explains, also, the spirit of those precautions which Joseph felt it prudent to take when it became needful to provide for the settlement of his brethren in Egypt. We refer particularly to his successful effort to get them assigned to a part of the country not only suited to their occupation, but where they could dwell apart from the Egyptians, and so, at least for a while, not arouse prejudice against themselves, either as foreigners or shepherds. It is easy enough to see, in view of all these circumstances, how neither Pharaoh nor his house nor the Egyptians would be apt to think of

danger in connection with the single family thus
allowed to live and thrive on Egyptian soil. And it
is but needful to suppose that during the remainder
of his life Joseph acted with the prudence of the
earlier years, to understand how his character would
continue to be respected, and his influence on behalf of his people's interests would be maintained
through every change of government he survived,
and as long as he lived ; and that only thereafter
could any suspicion and persecution of the Hebrews
begin.

The narrative of Joseph is indeed intensely Egyptian [1] in its whole spirit and in every detail, even to
names and places. It is as much so as the story of
Moses, whose Pharaoh is universally accepted as a
native sovereign. At any rate, the chronology that
obliges us to place Joseph's elevation in the reign
either of Thothmes III. or of Amenophis III. finds
this much confirmation in the fact that in either
case he would be an Egyptian king.

It may be added that either of them would be
also a great Pharaoh ; for such is also the impression
made by the Hebrew story. Joseph's Pharaoh was
a sovereign whose word was law, who could change
the very constitution of society in his realm, and
become in one sense a despot, though in another

---

[1] Brugsch's History, vol. i. p. 265. Ebers has entered into this question *in
extenso* in his books, and with his well-known insight and accuracy. Rev.
H. G. Tomkins also, in his valuable works, originally contributed as papers
to the "Victoria Institute."

sense, under Joseph's tuition, a really beneficent ruler. And curiously enough, this too was equally true of both the great Thothmes and the great Amenophis. The history of the monuments would show that both of these sovereigns were at once the most powerful and the most beneficent of Egypt's Pharaohs.

If the objection be urged to the identification of either of these Pharaohs as Joseph's Pharaoh, that there is no monumental indication [1] of Joseph's

[1] It would appear that there were two occasions, referred to on the monuments, when Egypt suffered from prolonged famines. Both, as was to be expected, have been claimed as the famine of Joseph's day. The first would carry us back, however, to the days of Usertesen I., the second king of Dynasty XII. (See Brugsch's " History," vol. i. p. 135 ; also "Records of the Past," vol. xii. p. 63.) This era is one in which some have located Abraham, but to which no one would now assign Joseph.

The other famine is mentioned by Brugsch (vol. i. p. 261). It is found in an inscription in the tomb of one Baba, whom Brugsch would synchronize with the period of the Rasekenens, one of whom, the first, was Apepi's contemporary. Brugsch, who regards Apepi as Joseph's Pharaoh, believes that in this instance the famine alluded to is that of Joseph's day ; and he regards Baba as an officer of the native prince, who acted under the instructions of Apepi, his suzerain, or of Joseph, Apepi's chief. But according to the chronology of the era as determined by both the Hebrew and Egyptian registers, Apepi must be considered as an impossible Pharaoh of Joseph, but may have been Abraham's Pharaoh. So that if Brugsch is right in his surmise that Baba was Apepi's contemporary, there may, curiously enough, be in his tomb-inscription an allusion to the famine that brought Abram to Egypt. The monuments, therefore, thus far yield no allusions to Joseph's famine.

There is, however, a monumental allusion to a granary officer in a subsequent reign who occupies a position so like Joseph's that one is certainly tempted at first thought to identify the two, and particularly as his Pharaoh was Amenophis III. M. Naville first directed attention to him in a letter dated Jan. 23, 1880. It is to be found in " Trans. Vict. Instit.," vol. xiv., appended to Rev. H. G. Tomkins' paper on " The Life of Joseph." M. Naville describes some pictures (see Prisse d'Avenne's " Monuments," Pl. XXXIX.– XLII.), which, as he says, reminded him strongly of Joseph and his employ-

presence in either reign, nor a hint even of any event of the fourteen-year period, it can only be replied, Not as yet. For the monumental history of the two reigns, while reasonably full, remains incomplete. But the objection would be of equal force with respect to the reign of any other supposed Pharaoh of Joseph. There were other famines in Egypt, — doubtless prolonged seasons of scarcity, — but there is monumental information of but two of them; and this has reached us, not on

ment. A minister named "Khaemha" stands in the presence of Amenophis III., while all others bow before him, showing that he is of exalted rank. He speaks to the king, and has under his command all the tax-gatherers and all that concerned the granaries. He has the strange title, " The eyes of the king in the towns of the South and his ears in the provinces of the North," which, as M. Naville says, implies that he knew the land perfectly, and that, like Joseph, he had *gone throughout all the land of Egypt* (Gen. xli. 46). " His resemblance with Joseph I find particularly striking, considering that Joseph seems to have been a purely civil officer, and to have had nothing to do with the military class." Mr. Tomkins was impressed with a scene in one of the pictures where the great man is decorated with a royal collar of gold, the gift of the king, just as was the case with Joseph.

It is to be remembered that both M. Naville and Mr. Tomkins make Apepi to be Joseph's Pharaoh, so that it was impossible for them to regard this "Khaemha" of Amenophis III. as Joseph. They were simply impressed with the resemblances between the two as illustrating the Scripture story. When, however, as seen already, we know that Amenophis III. could be the Pharaoh of Joseph's elevation, or at least that Joseph was his contemporary, it is certainly tempting to identify "Khaemha" as Joseph. But there is one reason that would utterly forbid the identification, — a fact not alluded to by either M. Naville or Mr. Tomkins, but which Plate XLII. makes clear, — that the great "Khaemha" is represented as offering first-fruits to the goddess Rannu, the patroness of the field and the garden. However one may believe that Joseph could have countenanced in any degree the purer sun-worship of the Heliopolite school, it could scarcely be credited that he conformed to the Egyptian usages as respects the other gods of the pantheon. So that it would seem to be necessary to disallow any identification of " Khaemha" as Joseph.

Levi.

Joseph    2                          I 0

180

2 0

0          4                 0      4 0

40                          8

hothmes III.    ah | S. II | Amenmes | Siptah | archy & Setnekht | Rameses III.

8   2   5   7         30          34

6

ns | A. II | T. IV | Amen | S. II | A. | Sipt | iarchy & Setnekht | Ram

54   7   7    20   4   5   7

38

othmes III = eptah      A | Siptah | Anarchy & Setnekht. | Rameses III

20   2   5   7    16         34

2 6

67   8

III        A II ineptah

54         20

any royal monument, but discovered by the merest accident in private tombs. Granting to the objection, however, its utmost force, it does not militate against the fact that not only the era of Joseph, but of the Hebrews taken as a whole, does fit itself, at many points of contact, into the history of Egypt authenticated by the monuments, and in a very satisfactory way. We have been reviewing the history of Joseph. We are next to deal with the era of Abraham, and then of Moses. And we will reach, we trust, some important conclusions. Still, the work of comparison has not been ended. It is only begun; but as far as the monuments at present allow us to go, the comparison in no particular reflects upon, but the rather supports, the Hebrew tradition. No one can say what more any day may bring to light. We must be grateful for the light we possess, and wait patiently for more.

## LECTURE IV.

### ABRAHAM AND MOSES.

THE Hebrew tradition[1] mentions a brief visit to Egypt made by Abraham ; and the question is therefore a natural one, whether its date can be fixed in the Egyptian chronology. Its precise date in the Hebrew time-period is not mentioned. It can only be approximately gathered, but near enough for our purpose. According to the Genesis story, the visit was made not very long after Abram had crossed " the River," and certainly before he had been ten years in the land of Canaan. One cannot, indeed, be far out of the way in supposing that it was made somewhere between the second and the fifth year of the Canaanitish sojourn ; for that would allow sufficient time for Lot's subsequent settlement in the Jordan valley, and the battle of the kings, all of which happened, it is clear, before the specified tenth year, when Abram took Hagar to wife.[2] If the visit was made then, somewhere between the second and the fifth year of the Hebrew time-

---

[1] Gen. xii. 10 to end, and xiii. 1, 2.
[2] Gen. xvi. 3. Compare verse 16.

period, it requires but a glance at the comparative chart of the two chronologies to observe that the visit must have been made while the Shepherds ruled Egypt ; for the fifth year of the Hebrew time-period coincides, in the adopted Egyptian Register (Register I.), with a year of the Shepherd Era which was, indeed, some eighty-five years previous to the Expulsion.

The question may therefore be asked, whether such a conclusion would find any support in the Hebrew and Egyptian stories. To this question it may be replied at once, that as far as the Hebrew story is concerned, there is nothing that would militate against such a conclusion, but the rather everything to favor it. An unprejudiced reader of Genesis can hardly fail to observe the difference between the Egypt of Abraham and the Egypt of Joseph, — a difference that cannot adequately be explained by the simple lapse of time. It is at once clear that the Pharaoh who received and so hospitably treated Abram, notwithstanding that he brought with him his flocks for keep, was an entirely different style of man from the king who shared with his people a hatred of foreigners, and particularly of the shepherd class. And while those who push back Abram into Dynasty XII., and so are obliged to reconcile the Hebrew story with a native reign, have found in the monumental history of native Pharaohs evidence to show that strangers were

allowed to enter and to dwell in Egypt, all must
admit that these are exceptions to the rule, and that
the Egyptians had as much contempt for foreigners
as the Chinese of our own day. Outside peoples
were looked upon as barbarians, to be tolerated,
if need be, within their borders, not hospitably entertained. What a contrast with this does the Genesis story present! There is a cordiality that marks
the reception of Abram with his herds, a simplicity
that characterized the relations between him and
Pharaoh and his princes, a tenderness of treatment
even amid the plagues occasioned by Abram's
prevarication, that one can hardly connect with a
proud and arrogant Egyptian prince. All is easily
enough explained if, as the comparison of the two
chronologies would suggest, he were a Shepherd
king, himself a Semitic or at least a foreigner.

If it be asked who he was, one can of course only
conjecture. And yet it would be a supposition in
whose favor much can be said, scrutinizing the two
chronologies, if we should suspect him to be the
very Apepi (or Apophis) that a Manetho tradition
made the Pharaoh of Joseph.[1] Considering the
confusions and misplacements that afflict so many
of the Manetho lists, it is perfectly possible that it
was a simple inadvertence in quoting the tradition,
that substituted Joseph's name for Abram's. For if
the Hebrew time-period be correctly dated from the

---

[1] Lepsius' Königsbuch, middle section, Dynasty XVII. (Eusebius' List).

calling of Abram, it is impossible that Joseph could have lived in Apepi's time, while it might be true of Abram.

Moreover, as far as the Egyptian chronology is concerned, the eighty-fifth year previous to the Shepherd Expulsion could very readily fall in the reign of Apepi. It has been stated already that the monuments establish the fact, suggested also by the Manetho lists, that the Shepherd kings of Dynasty XVII. were really suzerains, and that they recognized a native line as vassal princes. We may now add that it is possible to gather from the time-indications, imperfect as they are, which are available for the two lines, a quite satisfactory idea of the era of Apepi. With regard to the native line, e. g., the monuments prove that there were at least four princes in the native line previous to Aahmes, Egypt's liberator, — viz., three " Ta " princes, each also called " Sekenen Ra," and Kames, father of Aahmes. Then, as to the contemporary Shepherd line, the Manetho lists indicate that there were two, if not three of them, that intervened between the King Apepi who was suzerain to the first Ta (or Sekenen Ra) and the Shepherd king who was contemporary with Aahmes; for it is in this way only that Apepi's position in the Manetho lists can be explained.

As to the time covered by these contemporary suzerains and vassals, it can be said that while it is impossible to be certain as to this, it can nevertheless be approximately gathered.

It is certain, e. g., as to the native line, that Kames' reign was short,[1] but. as to the three " Ta " princes one can only conjecture. It is unknown whether they were father, son, and grandson, or father and two sons. If Maspero's surmise is correct, judging from the appearance of his mummy, the third Ta was about forty years old when struck down in battle.[2]

As to the regnal periods of the contemporary Shepherds, we are completely dependent on the Manetho lists ; and these, as is usual with the Manetho numbers, are in great confusion. Still, six out of the eight lists give Apepi sixty-one years ; and while the variations respecting the two or three which follow are considerable, it is at least clear that eighty-five years previous to the Expulsion would be' sure to bring us into some year of Apepi's reign. Beyond any doubt, the same period would be ample to bridge the interval in the native line between Ta I. (Sekenen Ra), who was Apepi's contemporary, and Aahmes, who expelled the Shepherds.

---

[1] Brugsch's History, vol. i. p. 252.   Chabas' Les Pasteurs, p. 41.

[2] In the "Academy" of July 31, 1886, may be found Maspero's detailed account of the unwrapping of the mummy.   It was among the "find" at Deir-el-Bahari.   The mummy is that of a man about forty and of a vigorous frame. Serious wounds, particularly one inflicted on his head with a mace, show that he was struck down in battle.   There was also some delay in securing his body ; for the embalming was done only after decomposition had set in, and all was done in haste.

Calculating the probabilities in this way from the meagre data available, one would certainly be justified in putting Abram's visit to Egypt in Apepi's time, and before the war of liberation had begun.

There is, moreover, a Scripture fact that certainly serves to corroborate the view that Abram's Pharaoh was at least a Shepherd king. We refer to the Divine prohibition that forbade Isaac to go to Egypt.

We learn from Gen. xxvi. 1, 2, that there was a famine in Isaac's as well as in Abram's day, and that Isaac was minded at first to seek relief in Egypt, but that " the Lord appeared unto him and said, Go not down into Egypt; dwell in the land which I shall tell thee of."

Why, it may be asked, was it deemed inexpedient just then for Isaac to seek an asylum in Egypt?

The precise date of the prohibition can only be approximately gathered, but it would seem from its position in the narrative to have been not long before Esau's marriage, which would make Isaac at the time about 100 years old. That date would be the one hundred and twenty-fifth year of the Hebrew time-period, which date in the Egyptian Register I. would coincide with the fortieth year after Aahmes' accession, or thirty-five years after the expulsion of the Shepherds.

There is no need, however, of fixing with greater precision the date of the occurrence, in either the

Hebrew or the Egyptian chronology. It is enough
to perceive that at the date of the prohibition the
Shepherds were no longer in the land, and to gather,
as can be done from the Egyptian history of the
years thereafter, that the spirit of enmity towards
the hated foreigners and all that would remind one
of them not only survived through all those years,
but became intensified. It was simply awaiting its
opportunity for revenge, — an opportunity that did
not come until the time of Thothmes III., when the
great " war of vengeance," as it was called, against
the Asiatics broke out, and only came to an end in
the complete subjugation of the peoples as far as the
Euphrates. Long after Isaac's time Joseph discovered that the feeling against the Shepherds was still
dominant among the Egyptians.

Amid such hate and spite surely it was not safe at
any time from the date of the Expulsion to Thothmes' own day for an Asiatic to be found in Egypt,
much less for one such to repair thither with flocks
and herds.

So that in the Divine prohibition laid upon Isaac
not to go thither, even under stress of famine, we
may find confirmation, albeit incidental, of the general correctness of the adopted chronology, suggesting on the one hand that Joseph's era was certainly
subsequent to the Shepherd Expulsion, and on the
other hand that Abraham's Pharaoh must have been
a Shepherd.

There is yet further corroboration of the surmise that Abram's Pharaoh was a Shepherd king in the fact mentioned by the sacred writer, that when Abram came into the land of Canaan he found not only "the Canaanite in the land," but, more specifically still, the Amorite and the Hittite, and, what is yet more noteworthy, a settlement of Hittites around Hebron.[1]

Modern research seems to have settled the point [2] that the original home of the Hittites was in the Southern Caucasus and in Cappadocia and some other parts of Asia Minor, and that they thence spread by way of Cilicia into Northern Syria, founding there an empire. Their principal capitals, as late as Dynasties XVIII. and XIX., were Carchemish on the Euphrates and Kadesh on the Orontes.[3] Northern Syria seems to have continued to be the habitat of the "Khita" as late as the time of Rameses II. There is no monumental evidence that the Khita inhabited Palestine earlier than that date.[4] It is on this ground, indeed, that some have disallowed the identification of the Hittites of Genesis with the monumental Khita, or regard them at least as Hittites of another stock.

[1] Gen. xii. 6; xiv. 13; xv. 16; xxiii. 10.

[2] Maspero's Histoire, p. 179.

[3] Wright's Empire of the Hittites (2d ed.).

[4] Brugsch's "History," vol. ii. p. 3; also Professor Sayce's "A New Hittite Inscription," in the "Academy" of Oct. 23, 1886, and criticisms thereon in the "Academy" of October 30, by Professor Cheyne and Dr. Neubauer; also Professor Sayce's reply, November 6; also Rev. H. G. Tomkins in the "Academy," Nov. 13, 1886.

But the presence of those Hittites in Southern
Palestine at so early a date is sufficiently well ex-
plained· by the modern theory which Maspero[1] and
others have developed, and which connects those
Hebron Hittites with a great migration which ended
only in the Shepherd Invasion of Egypt.

Maspero regards the migration as a Canaanitish
movement, others as a Semitic wave ; but both sides
hold that in trending southward from the starting-
point it either pushed forward or dragged along in
its train some of the Hittites and Amorites, who had
by that time occupied Northern Syria, and who were
in the path of the migration.    Palestine itself was already occupied by many other sons of Canaan, and
these were obliged to take refuge principally in
mountain fastnesses.    Now, according to the theory,
the great bulk of the emigrants pushed on and in-
vaded Egypt; but some of the fragmentary Hittite
and Amorite tribes stopped on the way, and were
left behind in Southern Palestine, scattered among
the original Canaanitish tribes.    Some of these tar-
ried in the vicinity of Hebron, and founded there a
town.    And the famous Numbers passage[2] would
seem to teach that these Hittites built Hebron some
seven years before the main body of emigrant invaders, who continued on their way, founded Zoan
in Egypt.

[1] Histoire, p. 161 et seq.
[2] Num. xiii. 22.

It is not necessary to infer from the 'Numbers passage, as some have done, that the Shepherds were Hittites. There are many reasons for believing with Brugsch that they were Semitics.[1] The connection between the two cities in the mind of the Numbers writer probably was, not that they were necessarily founded by the same race, but were the first-fruits of one and the same migration. But it will be perceived that the very presence of a few Hittites in Southern Palestine as early as Abram's day, when the real home of the Khita much later on was still in Northern Syria, would show, if any confidence is to be placed in the theory referred. to, that the Shepherd Invasion had already occurred when Abram came to Hebron.

As such, therefore, it is a valuable hint, in its chronological bearing, which the sacred writer gives when, once and again, we are told that in going through the land Abram found therein, not simply Canaanites, which would not have been so decisive, but Amorites, and particularly " sons of Heth," and that he found a home of the latter at Hebron.

There can, therefore, scarcely remain a doubt that the invaders were already in Egypt when Abram came into Palestine, just as the chronology of Register I. would indicate ; and the conclusion is then irresistible that his Pharaoh was a Shepherd king.

[1] History, vol. i. p. 198.

We need not dwell on the yet further confirmation of the conclusion thus reached, which the " Set Era " of the Tanis tablet furnishes.

Accepting the tablet as yielding a genuine Shepherd era, whose four hundredth year was the first or the fifth year of the sole reign of Rameses II., and whose initial year was the first year of Salatis of the Manetho lists, it is easy enough, comparing the two chronologies, to find its points of contact with the Hebrew time-period. And it will be found that the first year of Salatis coincided with the fifty-ninth year before Abram's seventy-fifth year; so that Abram at that date must have been still living in Ur, and was but sixteen years old. And accordingly the Semitic migration, which issued in the Shepherd Invasion, must have started on its way about the time of Abram's birth.

The " Set Era " thus curiously enough confirms the correctness of the interpretation that dates the Hebrew time-period from the calling of Abraham, and also points to Abram's Pharaoh as a Shepherd king.

In view, therefore, of the many circumstances all pointing one way, we can scarcely avoid the conclusion that Abram's Pharaoh was a Shepherd.

Turning now to the remaining interval of the Hebrew time-period, — viz., that between the death of Joseph and the Exodus, — it will be interesting to note its points of contact with the Egyptian chronology of Register I. At the outset attention may be drawn to the way in which the Hebrew writer would lead us to infer that no marked change occurred in the status of the Hebrew people as long as Joseph lived, nay, as long as Joseph's brethren lived, nor indeed as long as what he styles "that generation" lived. It is therefore a curious fact, in this connection, that the age of but one of Joseph's brethren, Levi, should have been preserved in the Levitical Registers. It is as though that life was an important link in the chain of life. This was the case, indeed, from several points of view. It is an important factor, e. g., as stated in the second lecture, in determining the question how the Hebrew time-period must be measured. It may now be said to be an equally important factor in its bearing on the special point before us; for the chart shows that if the chronology of Register I. can be trusted, Levi survived the accession of Seti I. one year. It is even possible that Levi was born two, or as many as four, years before Joseph, instead of but one year, as adopted in the chart; in which case his death-year would coincide with the date of Seti's accession, or even with that of Rameses I. Now, if this be a mere coincidence, it is truly remarkable; for in either case it would be in such perfect accord with the data of both stories. For as to the Hebrew story, e. g., while it suggests that no special change occurred in the position of the Hebrews until all of Joseph's

generation passed away, it undoubtedly suggests that
no long interval elapsed between the end of Joseph's
generation and the accession of the " new" Pharaoh,
with whom came a marked change; and the chronology of Register I. would abundantly sustain that
suggestion.

Then, as to the Egyptian story, if the close of
Joseph's generation really coincided with the accession of Seti I. (and yet more with that of Rameses I.),
the Egyptian history would tell how " new " such a
Pharaoh was, and how he would regard any claim of
Joseph's people on the national gratitude, even if he
knew aught of Joseph's history.   He belonged to a
new Dynasty.   Its founder, Rameses I., reigned at
most but a very few years, it is probable not more
than two.[1]  The Dynasty was in no sense · a legitimate Dynasty, except that it was recognized by the
priests of the day as the only possible government.
A *de ʔfacto* government was perforce recognized as
one, *de jure*.   Rameses I. and Horus, the last king of
Dynasty XVIII., may have been brothers, as Brugsch
believes,[2] and both may have been sons of King Ai,
as he also suggests; but even thus Ai himself was
but a courtier to Amenophis IV., and, simply by con-
sent of the priests, mounted an empty throne.   Moreover, added to the irritations which the consciousness
of the " newness " of the Dynasty would occasion, it is

[1] Maspero's Histoire, p. 214.
[2] History, vol. i. p. 460, and vol. ii. p. 8.

to be remembered that Horus and Rameses I. were contemporaries of Amenophis IV. the Reformer king; and it is even possible that Seti himself was also living at the time, though young. That they were all out of sympathy with the religious revolution of the "Aten" king, is well known. It was Horus who re-established the old religion and dishonored Ameno-phis IV. and his monuments. He probably based his best claim for recognition on his religious partisan-ship. When, then, we recall the probable influence of Joseph on the establishment of that purer "Aten" worship, it can be understood how a would-be sym-pathizer with the old religious forms would be in-clined to persecute rather than to favor Joseph's people. At any rate, Seti I., if for any reason, political or otherwise, he desired to check the power and influence of the Hebrews, would be the very man who would feel no compunctions in doing so.

His "knowing not Joseph" can be taken literally, or to mean his entire ignoring of Joseph and his services to the State.

There is nothing, therefore, in Egyptian history or chronology that would forbid our regarding Seti I. (or even Rameses I.) as the Pharaoh under whom began the change in the status of the Hebrew people, — a change that went from bad to worse rapidly enough, until in the time of Rameses II. the Hebrews had become slaves, obliged to do such duty to the

State as slaves had to render.   They worked in quarries, — the most dreaded toil of Egypt.   They made bricks, they dragged stone, and they builded; and all under circumstances that made the burden of life intolerable.

It is now certain, at any rate, that it was under Rameses II., the son of Seti I., that the Hebrews built Pithom, one of the two special cities mentioned in Ex. i. 11 as built by them for Pharaoh as store-cities.   The discoveries of M. Naville, under the auspices of the " Egypt Exploration Fund," have settled that point beyond dispute.   And as that is so, it must also have been he who devised that cruel method of controlling the increase of the Hebrew population which in the providence of God issued in the finding of Moses by the Pharaoh's own daughter and in the adoption into the royal family itself of one of the Hebrew children.

To the objection some may urge, that the narrative suggests that the Pharaoh for whom the store-cities were built was the same as the " new king," it may be replied that this does not necessarily follow.   The sacred writer does not pretend to accentuate the different Pharaohs of the story with precision.   The narrative is concerned, not with the succession of the sovereigns, but with the spirit which actuated the whole Dynasty.   There is a parallel instance of the indifference of sacred writers to the succession of kings, in the story of the fall of Samaria that

issued in the Israelitish captivity. One reading the
seventeenth chapter of the Second Book of Kings
would be sure to imagine that the "king of Assyria"
of the fifth verse was the same as the king of the
sixth verse. But in point of fact this was not so.
The king of verse 5 was Shalmaneser; and the
king of verse 6 was Sargon, a usurper. The
writer was not ignorant of the fact, as some have
imagined, but was not concerned with the mere
historical succession. Similarly, in the story before
us, a study of the narrative with the help of chronological indications will reveal therein at least four
Pharaohs, and those not all immediate successors
one to another. The "new king" may easily,
therefore, have been Seti I. or even his father,
though it is certain that it was Rameses II. for
whom the cities were built, and in whose time
Moses was born and from whose face he fled in his
fortieth year.

The attempt to fix Moses' place in the Egyptian
chronology is made an easy task by the certain data
regarding his place in the Hebrew time-period furnished by the Levitical Registers. Moses' place in
the Hebrew time-period is as certain a time-factor
as is the place of Joseph.

Comparing then the two chronologies, it will not
be so very difficult to differentiate from the Hebrew
story the reigns of the Pharaohs to which the events
of Moses' life may be assigned.

(1) The first third of his life would seem to have fallen entirely in the long reign of Rameses **II.**

Register **I.** would indicate that Moses' birth occurred when Rameses was at least thirty-eight years old, and consequently when he had been reigning alone about nine years. He was old enough, four years previous to this date, to have sons in at least formal command of army corps; so that it is easy enough to understand how the " Pharaoh's daughter " who found and adopted Moses could be Rameses' own daughter. She was doubtless quite young, and her father may have looked on her adoption of the babe as a child's fancy, which there was no special reason to disallow.

(2) By the time Moses reached his fortieth year, the Hebrew date that for the time terminated his Egyptian career, Rameses **II.** would be about seventy-eight years old, with yet some eighteen years of life before him. Inordinately large as was his family, death had been busy among them; for the Pharaoh who really succeeded him was his thirteenth son! Rameses indeed associated this son Mineptah with himself on the throne some twelve years before his death; so that Moses fled from the face of Rameses about six years before Mineptah became colleague-Pharaoh. Attention may be drawn to this circumstance; for, considering Moses' peculiar history and the position he would occupy among the royal princes as the adopted son of Mineptah's sister, it

could scarcely happen that Mineptah should be ignorant of his flight, or that he would condone his
offence when he returned. But God testified to
Moses in Midian that "they were dead that sought
his life." Putting these circumstances together,
they would certainly exclude Mineptah as a possible
Exodus Pharaoh.

(3) It will be observed that Moses' eightieth year,
which the Hebrew story synchronizes with the Exodus date, is made by Register I. to coincide with the
close of Dynasty XIX., — not, be it observed, necessarily with the close of Siptah's reign, as the chart
suggests, but with the close of the third of the three
brief reigns after Mineptah (whatever the order of
succession may be), with which Pharaoh the Dynasty
ended and Anarchy began. This point will, however,
occupy us in the closing lecture, and so need not
detain us now.

(4) The one hundred and twentieth year of Moses
— the Hebrew date of his death, and the date that
concluded the period of the wandering and began the
period of the Palestine conquest and occupation — is
made to synchronize in Register I. with the tenth year
of Rameses III., — a date which, as will be seen in the
next lecture, is one of singular importance in our inquiry; for not until then, or at the very earliest not
until the year before, would it have been possible for
the Hebrews to have entered Palestine so well. In
this way it is possible to fit Moses' entire career, as

given in Hebrew story, to the Egyptian chronology
and history.

Before concluding, it may be well to draw attention to a single example of the way in which the
sacred writer, while not attempting (as has been
said) to accentuate the succession of Pharaohs with
precision, nevertheless makes no mistake in devel-
oping the progress of the story. We refer to the
statement of Ex. ii. 23, " And it came to pass in
process of time, that the king of Egypt died." Now,
most writers have considered that the reference here
is to the death of Rameses II., and then, jumping
to the conclusion that the next Pharaoh mentioned — the one to whom Moses was sent — must
consequently have been his son, have inferred
thence that Mineptah must have been the Exodus
Pharaoh. But it is only needful to compare the
two chronologies to see that this is a mistake. The
two chronologies would show that the reference
in verse 23 in all probability is not to Rameses
II. at all. The very form of expression, " *It came
to pass in process of time*, that the king of Egypt
died," would seem to imply that a considerable
time had elapsed since Moses' flight, — certainly a longer time than the eighteen years Register I. would
allow for the interval to the death of Rameses II.
Further, the narrative introduced by the passage in
question certainly suggests the near approach of the
end. The king who died, therefore, " in the process

of time," and so late on as to be quite near the
Exodus, may have been the second, or, as is more
likely, the third successor of Rameses II., but neither
Rameses himself nor Mineptah his son. The statement is made at all, to introduce a new chapter
in the story, and, as is evident, to mark one of its
later stages. It shows that lapse of time did not
mend matters, and that the death to which he
refers inaugurated a new stage of cruelty. The
connection implies that with the accession of the
new Pharaoh — i. e., the latest Pharaoh — there
was a superadded cruelty, which led the Hebrews
to cry mightily unto God, and which led God to
interfere.

The next lecture will deal with the date of the
Exodus, and attempt to identify it with the close
of Dynasty XIX. And Register I. indicates that the
Dynasty did not end with Mineptah, but with one of
three Pharaohs who followed him. Allowance must
accordingly be made for these three regnal periods;
and, allowance thus made, the conclusion must be
reached, that the passage in question did not refer
to Rameses II. at all. It is but necessary, indeed,
to properly weigh what is said of any Pharaoh in the
narrative, to perceive how any interval of time, and
any number of Pharaohs required by the Egyptian
chronology, can find room in the story.

In conclusion, we may say that the general harmony of the two stories is assured.

It only remains for us, now, to compare the two chronologies somewhat more carefully, so as to gather thence, if possible, a more precise indication as to the era of the Exodus, and who was its Pharaoh, — a task to which we will next address ourselves.

# LECTURE V.

## THE EXODUS ERA.

THE close of Dynasty XIX. is involved in almost as much obscurity as its rise. Uncertainty attaches not only to the regnal periods, but to the order of the succession, and so renders any argument based on the history of the Dynasty as yet but hypothetical. Accordingly, its history is variously handled by Egyptologists. All authorities, however, agree in the view that the Dynasty came to an end amid disaster and confusion. Were there no other ground for this view, the so-called "Great Harris Papyrus of Rameses III." would be sufficient to settle the point. It was found near Medinet-Abou,[1] and is dated the thirty-second year of Rameses III.

In the earlier part of the document Rameses recounts his good deeds, and commends to the people the son whom he was at the time associating on the throne. He then tells the story of his

---

[1] The Arabs who sold it to Mr. Harris refused to indicate the place of their "find." It is probable that it originally belonged to the royal library, but was hidden with other works in some extempore grotto for safety, and there remained until these last days.

own succession, prefacing this portion with a very brief but important statement respecting the period of anarchy that had been brought to an end by Setnekht his predecessor, now generally regarded as the founder of Dynasty XX.

Remembering the habitual reticence of the Egyptians respecting national disasters, the formal statement of the Harris Papyrus is certainly remarkable, and deserves more attention than it has already received. It cannot be a reminiscence, as some have imagined, of the Hyksos period, — for that came to an end, as is known, with the rise of Dynasty XVIII.; and according to the papyrus, the period to which it refers came to an end with the rise of Dynasty XX.

The date thus so explicitly assigned to it, coupled with a fair interpretation of its language, may not unfairly suggest, we believe, that we have in this papyrus of Rameses III. a veritable reference to the Hebrew Exodus.

The papyrus is a large one, measuring some 133 feet in length, admirably preserved, and is divided into seventy-nine leaves. Of these, the last five comprise the historical part so called; and it is simply the first paragraph of this historical part with which this inquiry is concerned.

The historical part of the papyrus was first translated and published by Dr. Eisenlohr in 1872.[1]   The

---

[1] Der grosse Papyrus Harris, Leipzig, 1872.

same year he read before the London ·" Society of Biblical Archæology " a paper " on the political condition of Egypt before the reign of Rameses III., probably in connection with the establishment of the Jewish religion." [1] This paper furnishes an English translation of the historical part of the papyrus.

In 1873–1874 Dr. Eisenlohr revised his translation of this part, and added a translation of the greater part of the papyrus.[2] The same year Dr. Birch published a translation of the first third of the document.[3] A complete translation of the papyrus will be found in the " Records of the Past," [4] under the joint authority of Drs. Eisenlohr and Birch.

In 1873 M. Chabas, in his " Recherches," [5] translates and discusses, in a very patient and scholarly way, the last five leaves, paragraph by paragraph, severely criticising Dr. Eisenlohr's renderings in many places. Dr. Brugsch, also, has given, in his " History of Egypt," [6] a translation of the historical portion.

Considering the possible bearing of " the important passages," as Brugsch calls them, on the Hebrew history, it will be well to compare these several translations. Dr. Eisenlohr's is his latest, as found in the " Records of the Past," coupled, indeed,

---

[1] In vol. i. of the Society's " Transactions."
[2] See " Zeitschrift " for 1873 and 1874.       [3] Idem, 1873.
[4] Vols. vi. and viii.       [5] Recherches, p. 9.
[6] History, vol. ii. p. 137.

with Dr. Birch's authority. This translation reads thus:[1] —

"The land of Kami had fallen into confusion. Every one was doing what he wished. They had no superior for many years who had priority over the others. The land of Egypt was under chiefs of nomes, each person killing the other for ambition and jealousy. Other events coming after it. Distressing years. A-ar-su a Kharu amongst them as chief. He placed the whole country in subjection before him . . . no offerings were made in the interiors of the temples."

Dr. Brugsch's translation is : —

"The people of Egypt lived in banishment abroad. Of those who lived in the interior of the land, none had any to care for him. So passed away long years, until other times came. The land of Egypt belonged to princes from foreign parts. They slew one another, whether noble or mean. Other times came on afterwards during years of scarcity. Arisu, a Phœnician, had raised himself among them to be a prince, and he compelled all the people to pay him tribute . . . the gods were treated like the men. They went without the appointed offerings in the temples."

Chabas' translation is : —

"It happened that the country of Egypt was (or, had been) thrust outside. To all who remained in its interior there was no master during numerous years in the beginning. During a time the Egyptian country belonged to Oerou,[2] governing the cities. It was extraordinary, surprising. Other times came afterwards for a few years.

---

[1] Vol. viii. p. 46.

[2] It means "governors," literally, "mouths," — i. e., men by whose "word" the people were ruled. Compare Gen. xli. 40.

Areos, a Syrian, was an Oer among them, and the whole country paid homage to him . . . and the gods became like men. Offerings were no more made in the temples."

It will at once be observed that the special part of the paragraph of the papyrus with which this review is concerned is simply the first sentences of the passage, — viz., those translated by Drs. Eisenlohr and Birch,

"The land of Kami had fallen into confusion. Every one was doing what he wished. They had no superior;"

and by Dr. Brugsch,

"The people of Egypt lived in banishment abroad. Of those who lived in the interior of the land none had any to care for him;"[1]

and by Chabas,

"It happened that the country of Egypt had been thrust outside. To all who remained in its interior there was no master."[2]

It will be observed that the translations of the clauses by Brugsch and Chabas quite agree, while that of Dr. Eisenlohr seems to be at best but a free translation. There is no wonder, therefore, that Brugsch should animadvert, as he does, on the labor

---

[1] The original in his "Geschichte Aegyptens" (Leipzig, 1877), p. 589, reads: "Das Volk von Aegypten lebte in der Verbannung im Auslande. Jedermann der im Innern des Landes geblieben war, entbehrte eines Fürsorgers."

[2] The original reads, "Il est arrivé, que l'Égypte s'était jetée au dehors;" or, literally, "fut le pays d'Égypte jeté au dehors."

of his predecessors, evidently alluding to Drs. Eisenlohr and Birch, affirming that "several of them had
completely mistaken the sense of the document just
in its most important passages."

There can be no doubt as to the general correctness of Brugsch's and Chabas' renderings, after examining the elaborate discussion the latter gives to
these two clauses of the papyrus, justifying, as he
does, his translation (of the first clause more partien-
larly) by numerous illustrations of the use of the
original words in a variety of connections, and translating the clause with as much precision as a literal
rendering can make of it.

He shows that the verb "khaa," which
he translates by "jeter" or "se jeter," has indeed
two meanings, — (1) "to throw, as in throwing
stones or to cast into the water;" and (2) "to leave,
forsake, quit." He also mentions, and with exam-
ples of its use in that sense, a secondary meaning of
"se jeter," — viz., "to throw one's self, to withdraw,
escape, flee;" so that, as he says, "we would not
therefore be too bold if we translated, *the country of
Egypt had fled outside*, for it is the veritable meaning
or intention of the phrase." And he concludes that
"the translation which indicates an emigration of
the Egyptian population is therefore founded on the
incontestable value of the Egyptian words; it is
also justified by the context," — referring to the next

clause, where distinct mention is made of those who remained in the country.

It should be added that Dr. Birch seems to have been so far influenced by Chabas' discussion as to have modified the view taken in the " Records of the Past;" for in his " History of Egypt"[1] he wrote : " The interval between the reign of Siptah and his successor Setnekht was one of great disturbance. From the ' Great Harris Papyrus ' it appears that *a great exodus* took place in Egypt. In consequence of the troubles *for many years*, it says, *there was no master.*"

It should also be added that the Hieroglyphic Dictionaries have adopted the two significations of the word urged by Chabas, — both the great Dictionary by Dr. Brugsch[2] and the smaller one of Pierret's, — as also a special Dictionary of this very papyrus by Dr. Piehl.

It should be mentioned, moreover, that none of the authorities quoted identify the papyrus " Exodus " with that of the Hebrews. The translation of the clauses insisted upon by Chabas, virtually agreed to by Dr. Brugsch, and apparently adopted by Dr.

---

[1] Page 136.

[2] In Brugsch's "Dict. Hiérog.," vol. iii. p. 1025, the verb "khaa" is assigned the two meanings, — (1) "to lay aside, cast away, reject ;" and (2) "to demit, relinquish."

In Pierret's " Vocab. Hiérog.," p. 391, he quotes Chabas, and gives, (1) "to put aside, throw, reject, or send away ;" (2) "to leave, quit."

In Dr. Karl Piehl's " Dict. du Pap. Harris, No. I." (Vienna, 1882), p. 69, he gives the two meanings, — " expulser, expatrier."

Birch may be accepted, therefore, with the greater confidence, because based on purely philological grounds.

Aside, therefore, from any specific reference of the papyrus, one will not certainly be far out of the way, if Chabas' conclusion be accepted, that the papyrus statement refers, however obscurely and indirectly, to an *" emigration from Egypt,"* for some reason, *" of a part of its population,"* — an emigration so large, compared with the population left behind, that those left behind were no longer able to hold the country.

The context would also suggest that the emigration was most disastrous in its effects upon the country. In some way those left behind found themselves without a legitimate head ; and as a consequence, government not only, but society as well, speedily resolved into confusion and anarchy. Then the document tells how the country was left a prey to its always envious neighbors, and how there resulted eventually a foreign despotism, which in turn was followed by a reaction, of which the papyrus speaks, in the shape of a national uprising, and how the end came in the re-establishment of a native Dynasty, in the person of one Seti the Victorious, Rameses' predecessor. It can scarcely be denied that such is a fair summary of the teaching of this very brief but suggestive narrative of the royal scribe of Rameses III.

. Do we then strain out of this document, in any illegitimate or forcible a way, a covert allusion to the Hebrew migration and its results ?

Beyond question, the Hebrew tradition adequately explains the story of Rameses.

(1) The Exodus of the Hebrew population of Egypt, "with the mixed multitude " that went out with them, was surely large enough to leave the northeast part of the Delta comparatively empty.

(2) The destruction of Pharaoh and of his chosen captains and horsemen would sufficiently account for the land of Egypt being left "without a head ; " rendering it needful, in the first instance, that each nome should look out for itself, just as the papyrus states, — a condition of things that would inevitably lead to the jealousies and ambitions of which the papyrus also speaks.

(3) History would simply repeat itself in the invasion story. No better opportunity for foreign intervention could be furnished than intestine struggles would afford.

(4) And history would also simply repeat itself in the re-establishment of the native line by a shrewd chief, ready to take advantage of his opportunities.

But this is not all. The propriety of referring to the Hebrew Exodus the passage of the papyrus may be justified, not only by a fair interpretation of the words and the possibility of harmonizing the two stories. It is also possible to synchronize the era of the papyrus narrative with the era of the Exodus and of the Palestine occupation.

To be sure, there is an element of uncertainty here, which the monuments have not yet removed, both as respects the order of the succession and the regnal periods of the closing third of Dynasty XIX. ; still it is possible, nevertheless, no matter what the true order of succession may be, and adopting for the regnal periods simply the years which all Egyptologists would allow, perfectly to effect the synchronism. Assigning to Mineptah either the eight monumental years or the twenty claimed by some, and giving to Seti II. his two monumental years or the four claimed for him, to Amenmes five, and to Siptah seven,[1] we then reach the era of anarchy, and then the subsequent re-establishment of the monarchy by Setnekht. And though the precise length of time occupied by these events cannot be stated, all Egyptologists would agree in allowing for the interval between the close of Dynasty XIX. and the accession of Rameses III. about thirty years, — a period certainly long enough and yet not too long.[2]

A glance at the chart will show that the fortieth year after the Exodus — i. e., the date of the Palestine occupation — would, on the basis of the chronology mentioned, coincide with the tenth year of Rameses

---

[1] Maspero in his "Histoire," p. 259, says of the Mineptah successors : "The Manetho lists seem to attribute to them all but a dozen years at most."

[2] This would abundantly cover the reign of Setnekht, which was not long, and the "many years" and "years after" of the papyrus story.

III., — a date whose importance and bearing on our inquiry a very slight acquaintance with the history of the reign will reveal.

It was in the eighth year of Rameses III., but two years previous, that occurred the war which, considered in its results to Egypt and to Palestine, may be regarded as a most marked providential preparation for the Hebrew occupation of the promised land.

The story of the war is written in full on Egypt's own monuments, and there is not a modern history of Egypt but furnishes a more or less detailed account of it.

Maspero may be said to have furnished a philosophical view of it,[1] though without the remotest application of it to the Hebrew story, or with even a hint that it could be so used. According to him, the eighth-year war of Rameses III. was in fact a life and death struggle between Egypt and a new power, — a great confederacy of Asia Minor tribes. It was really another wave of migration, comprising Danaens, Tyrseniens, Shakalash (the later Sicilians), Teucrians, Lycians, Pelasgians, and a host of other tribes.[2] Instead of passing on westward, they marched southward, conquering and almost annihilating the peoples through whose countries they journeyed. They took Northern Syria, and broke up into frag-

---

[1] Histoire, ch. vi.
[2] Chabas' Recherches, pp. 30-50 ; Brugsch's History, vol. ii. p. 147.

ments the great Hittite Empire, with which Egypt had made an alliance in the time of Rameses II., and with which it had maintained friendly relations all through that reign and Mineptah's and, as far as is known, until anarchy came.

The Hittites had gradually come to be the dominating power throughout Syria and Northern and Central Palestine, — the only people, indeed, whom the Egyptians seem to have regarded as their equal.

But the new power " completely disintegrated " the Hittite Empire, as Maspero says,[1] converting so much of it as survived the crash into a host of petty kingdoms without any central authority. Having done this, the wave rolled on towards Egypt, and by a concerted movement the attack was delivered by sea and by land.

Fortunately for Egypt, all this took time, and the long march gave Rameses time to receive them. The conflict, which was the turning-point of the war, took place in his eighth year, between Raphia and Pelusium, under the walls of a fortress called the tower of Rameses III. The victory fell to Rameses; and as a result, the confederacy of Asia Minor peoples was hurled back whence they came, and the wave of Asiatics, instead of emigrating to the Arabian peninsula and the African shores, as had been the fashion for centuries before, was obliged to go

---

[1] Histoire, p. 267. Compare Lenormant's Manuel, vol. i. p. 297.

westward, ultimately peopling a good part of the European peninsulas, especially Italy and the islands, where they became the prehistoric and historic peoples with which all are now familiar.

But can one help seeing how the Asia Minor migration, that so effectually broke the backbone of the great Hittite Empire, really prepared the way for the entrance into Palestine of the Hebrews under Joshua, and for the easier conquest and occupation of the land?

Undoubtedly, it adequately explains the phenomena which the Hebrew tradition makes so evident, of the almost numberless petty tribes, with their several chiefs, that could all be called "Hittites" or by other Canaanitish names, which Joshua set himself to conquer.

Moreover, as all historians agree, Rameses needed no more to conduct in person a campaign in that direction. That great victory of his eighth year did not end his wars. He had another in his eleventh year; but it was in the West, against the Libyans, who were aided by some of those same Asia Minor peoples, who seem to have fled for safety in their ships to the Libyan coasts. But they met with such a defeat that the Libyans never after disturbed Egypt.

Rameses III. also had a campaign, a naval one, against the Arabians, and some minor expeditions into the Sinaitic peninsula, whereby he restored to the realm those ancient mining-districts. It should be observed, in passing, that the very fact shows that they had been lost to Egypt; and, moreover, it is clear that by that time the Hebrews had been long out of the way. In a few years Rameses was able to reconstitute the dominion of Egypt to proportions it had not known, certainly since the time of Seti II. We say Seti II.; for it is curious to know, what is assured by the monuments, that the Egypt of Rameses II., as respects the eastern Delta and its Syrian relations, continued to be the Egypt not only of Mineptah but of Seti II., his son. There is nothing all through those years to indicate the slightest trouble at home or in their foreign relations, at least in that direction, during those two reigns.

It is because of such facts as these that so many feel compelled to give up the view that Mineptah was the Exodus Pharaoh. It was not, as far as known, until the disaster occurred, whatever it may have been, that inaugurated the anarchy of the Harris Papyrus, that any change occurred in Egypt's relations with the East. Rameses III. found the Syrian province gone, and Bedouins to the east of the Delta contending for its possession. Even after the victory of his eighth year, he seems to have been content with the result that hurled back the new Asiatics whence they came; for he seems to have maintained only a semblance of authority on the eastern Mediterranean coast, simply maintaining

garrisons there. Crushed by the Italo-Greek invaders, as some call them, from their ultimate locale,
and impressed by Rameses' great victory, the Syrians
made no concerted effort for independence, and the
petty tribes in Palestine proper found enough to
do in contesting with the Hebrews the possession
of that land. If there were disturbances of the bal-
ance of power on the coast or elsewhere, these were
but partial and temporary, and they were easily
enough reduced by the generals in the neighboring
garrisons. As Chabas says, Rameses III. "did not
put these small conflicts among his victories, because
he was not there in person ; but they do explain the
presence of a Khitan chief and an Amorite chief in
the pictures portraying nations subjugated."

It may be added that the state of things thus
described can also explain the fact that some
"Aperiu" are mentioned in the reign of Rameses
III., — i. e., some "Hebrews," if one may identify the
two names. One argument against the identification,
for which so much may be said,[1] urged by those who
disallow it, is that a band of "Aperiu" are mentioned
in this reign and in that of Rameses IV., it being
alleged that this could not be if the "Aperiu" be
"Hebrews." But all becomes clear enough by bearing in mind the relations Rameses III. sustained with
Palestine and the Syrian peoples. It can be under-

---

[1] For a discussion of the identification of the "Aperiu" with the Hebrews,
see the special "Essay on the Aperiu" appended to these Lectures.

stood that if Rameses' generals could capture a Hittite and an Amorite chief, they could also capture
some Hebrews, in a possible conflict or intervention.
This explanation is, moreover, the more probable,
because the " Aperiu " of both Rameses III. and IV.
are described as war captives, those of the latter even
as " bowmen," whereas the " Aperiu " of Rameses II.
are pictured simply as foreign slaves.

Taking the data of these years, however, that are
unquestionable, how well do they fit in with the
Hebrew time-period?  There are, indeed, not only
the general arguments, already referred to sufficiently, that would point to the tenth, or even the
ninth, year of Rameses III. as the earliest possible
date when the Hebrews could cross into Palestine,
but there are incidental details that neatly fit into
both stories, — e. g., (1) The date of the reconquest
by Rameses III. of the mining regions of the Sinaitic
peninsula, when the Hebrews could not possibly have
been near; (2) The existence of the Amorite tribes
that faced Moses and the Hebrews at Kadesh,[1] — the
very position that could well enough give trouble to
an Egyptian garrison.  It is therefore certainly more
than a mere coincidence that an Amorite chief
should be among the chiefs captured by Rameses'
generals.  (3) The peculiar significance, in view of
the history recounted, of the description given (Josh.
i. 4) of the promised land the Hebrews were about

[1] Deut. i. 7, compared with verses 19, 20, and 41–46.

to enter, as "the land of the Hittites." The phrase but a year or two before would have struck terror into the minds of the Israelites. When uttered by Joshua, it does not sound so formidable. It is as though he said, "the land that was, but is no longer, the' Hittites' land," referring to the utter disintegration of the once great empire by the Asiatic invaders.

Thus, on philological and historical grounds, it is equally possible to maintain that in the brief story of the Harris Papyrus there was a veritable reference to the Hebrew migration. There is not an incident of the era, as told by the Hebrew narrator, that is inconsistent with the state of things suggested by the Rameses' story. Mention may be made of even so small an incident as the question whether the Hebrews fled or were thrust out. Both were true in point of fact; and, curiously enough, the Egyptian word of the papyrus, "khaa," as Chabas shows, may have either or both meanings. As far as that word is concerned, the people to whom it refers may have been "thrust out" or may have "thrust themselves out." If it be suggested that the allusion of the papyrus, though a possible allusion to the Hebrew Exodus, is but indirect and not decisive, it may be replied that it was not to be expected that any allusion at all, much less a distinct mention of the misfortune, would be made on an Egyptian monument. The Egyptians could scarcely be expected to perpetuate on their walls or inscribe on a papyrus roll an account of a disaster. As is well known, allusions to even the Shepherd conquest and domination are but few, and those most indirect and uncertain of explanation. Nevertheless, the allusion in the Harris Papyrus is clear enough. It is perfectly applicable to the Hebrew Exodus, but to no other known event of that era.

Further, if it be wondered at that but a single copy of this invaluable State document should have reached our day, it may be said that it was simply a good Providence that preserved this single copy to Egyptology; for it came near being destroyed by an explosion near Mr. Harris' house in Alexandria, that seriously damaged other manuscripts. The Arab excavators who sold the document to Mr. Harris in 1856 showed him a sack full of papyri that, as they affirmed, were found in the same place. Unfortunately, he was able to buy but a few of them, among them being the so-called "Harris Magic Papyrus." As Chabas says, "What has become of the rest?—a sack full of papyri, how many problems might have been solved!"

It may be mentioned also, in explanation of the rarity of any monumental reference to the anarchy of the papyrus, that we may be thankful that Rameses III. felt it to be needful to mention it at all; else we might have had no monumental reference whatever to it. He had good reason for mentioning it. He was associating his son upon the throne, being anxious to secure the succession.[1] He did not feel his tenure of the crown to be so secure as to require no justification. His reference, therefore, to the circumstances under which Setnekht mounted the throne, to which he himself succeeded, was really an appeal to both the gratitude and the fears of the nation.

Not, however, to delay on these points, there is beyond question good reason to believe that the papyrus alludes, and distinctly enough, to the Hebrew migration. Such a reference is justified by a fair interpretation of its language, by its chronology, by its general agreement with the Hebrew tradition, and, it may be added, by the impossibility of referring the Rameses' story to any purely Egyptian emigration from Egypt, of that or indeed of any other era.

Before concluding, allusion may be made to the different way in which Maspero interprets both the allusion of the Rameses' story and the Hebrew tradition. Instead of seeing in the Hebrew Exodus an adequate explanation of the anarchy of which the papyrus speaks, Maspero sees in the Exodus simply a consequence of the anarchy. He says [2] that " one can easily understand how, in the midst of general disorder, a foreign persecuted tribe should quit its

---

[1] He lived but two years afterward.
[2] Histoire, p. 262.

quarters and gain the desert highway without being energetically combated by its ancient masters, themselves too menaced to trouble themselves much about the flight of a band of slaves." We quote this at length, because it is a fair example of that free criticism of Scripture facts in which many writers indulge. The Bible story reveals no such period of internal disorder previous to the Exode, but rather a government undisturbed, albeit tyrannical. Moreover, Israel's Exode, strictly considered, was not a flight but a thrusting out, although Pharaoh did soon change his mind, and did feel it to be worth while "energetically" to combat the departing band of slaves. This Pentateuchal story is, moreover, in precise accord with the papyrus story. Maspero's version of the Exodus certainly receives no countenance from the Egyptian scribe. That papyrus is a veritable state document, and, interpreted fairly, tells of an emigration from Egypt of some of its inhabitants, and, if language means anything, also tells us that the prolonged anarchy quelled by Setnekht was a *consequence* of that emigration. It cannot, without violence to the construction, be considered as teaching that the emigrants took advantage of an era of confusion.

The two traditions point therefore to the same sequence of events, — the disaster, whatever it was, came first; confusion ensued. It is certainly refreshing to find, therefore, that on so many grounds it is possible to identify the Egyptian emigration as the veritable Hebrew Exodus. There is no need to cast aspersions on the Hebrew tradition, nor on the Hebrews.

It should be stated that Maspero was not indulging in any formal criticism of the papyrus. He was combatting the view that looks upon Mineptah as the Pharaoh of the Exodus. He was seeking to identify Seti II., with whom he ends the Dynasty, as that Pharaoh. He knew that the period of the three brief reigns following Mineptah's was an era of contested successions, and he finds "only in the years that precede and follow Seti II. conditions favorable to an Exode." He looks on that era as one of confusion, to which he could refer the papyrus language; amid which confusion, he imagines, the Hebrews, seizing their chance, departed.

But not only, as we have seen, does the Harris Papyrus really tell another story; the Egyptian history itself, as respects those closing reigns of Dynasty XIX., will not support Maspero's view. There is an order of succession of the three Pharaohs, which we may venture to call the monumental order and for which much may be said, that will equally avoid the need of identifying Mineptah as the Exodus Pharaoh, and of regarding the Exodus as occurring in an era of confusion, — an order, it is claimed, that may be made in a remarkable way to harmonize with both the monuments and the Hebrew tradition. And to this final point we devote our last lecture.

## LECTURE VI.

### THE EXODUS PHARAOH.

WHICH king it was who thrust the Hebrews out of Egypt, is still a matter of conjecture. It can be said, however, that during the past few years the problem has been brought within narrower limits.

Until recently Egyptologists have been divided as to even the Dynasty of the Exodus Pharaoh ; some being strongly in favor of assigning him to Dynasty XVIII., while others, following De Rougé's lead, preferred Dynasty XIX.[1] Happily, the labors of the Egypt Exploration Fund Committee have decided the question as between the two Dynasties.

It was M. Naville, the Committee's able explorer, who, while unearthing the mounds at Tel-el-Maskhuta, had the good fortune to discover that they covered the long-sought store-city Pithom, one of the two such towns built for Pharaoh by the Hebrews. And he was able, by the evidence of monuments found upon the spot, to connect the place in a very convincing way with Rameses II. of Dynasty XIX. as

[1] Report on Egyptian Studies, 1867, p. 27.

its founder, proving beyond appeal that Rameses II. was one at least of the Pharaohs who oppressed the Hebrews.[1]

Accordingly, the Exodus story must be harmonized, if it is ever to be done, with the era of Dynasty XIX. And the practical question, therefore, to be answered is, whether it is at present possible to gather from the monumental history of that Dynasty any hint as to who the Exodus Pharaoh must have been.

In the last lecture the attempt was made to identify the Exodus as the disaster which brought Dynasty XIX. to a close, and which, according to the "Great Harris Papyrus," inaugurated that period of anarchy which Setnekht, founder of Dynasty XX., brought to an end.

It is evident, therefore, that the question of this lecture will be answered if we can ascertain who the last Pharaoh of Dynasty XIX. really was.

[1] See Naville's "Pithom," pp. 11-13. Lepsius, in the "Zeitschrift" for 1883, Part II., published an article in which he declined to admit M. Naville's identification, and restated his old view of the positions of Pithom and Rameses. The article was really a too early reply to a simple letter of Naville's, in which he scarcely did more than announce his discovery. Nobody doubts that had Lepsius lived to see the multiplied proofs for the identification gathered in the Committee's first Memoir, he would have been convinced as others have been. No other Egyptologist of eminence has combated the identification. Brugsch early gave his adhesion to it, though it obliged him to give up a pet theory (see two articles of his, one in the "Deutsches Revue," Berlin, for October, 1883, and the other in the number for March, 1884). Ebers also cordially accepts it (see "Zeitschrift," 1885, Part II.). A translation of Ebers' article may be found in the "Academy," May 23, 1885. W. Pleyte also accepts the discovery (see "Academy," June 6, 1885). The French Egyptologists have also given in their adhesion, voiced by the eminent Eugene Revillout (see his letter to the "Academy," April 4, 1885).

It has been already stated that an element of uncertainty remains as to the order of succession of the last three Pharaohs with whom the monuments seem to close Dynasty XIX., — viz., Seti II., Amenmes, and Siptah.

Egyptologists agree that Amenmes preceded Siptah, but they differ as to the position to be assigned to Seti II., — whether he is to be placed before or after the other two; in other words, whether he should be regarded as immediate successor to Mineptah or should close the Dynasty.

At best, therefore, it can only be affirmed at present, by those who reject Mineptah as the Exodus Pharaoh,[1] that he must have been either Seti II. or Siptah.

[1] The reign of Mineptah is sufficiently well indicated on the monuments. Chabas, in his "Recherches" (p. 79 et seq.), has industriously gathered every known fact and hint respecting him.

There are monuments of the time when he was yet crown prince, and others of his associated reign with his father, and others still of his reign when his son Seti II. was but crown prince ; so that the general character of the reign can be regarded as settled. The monuments, indeed, amply illustrate his reign from its first to its eighth year, with which it probably closed. He was no longer young when he began his sole reign. Maspero ("Histoire," p. 255) says he must have been sixty. Nothing seems to have occurred within or without its borders in his day that affected the realm. The peace with the Hittites was maintained. He had a critical war in his fifth year with the Libyans in the West ; but he was victor, and the eastern Delta remained quiet. His subsequent reign was peaceful. In the Northeast he maintained the garrison posts, even in the land of Amori, and was constantly engaged in peaceful labors. Two papyri of his eighth year show that the relations between the Delta and Syria were still undisturbed. The same can be said of the condition of Egypt under the administration of his son, who succeeded him. Seti was indeed associated on the throne before Mineptah's death, and there is not a hint of trouble or disaster. The transition from father to son reveals no change. The first-born of Pharaoh that was destroyed on the night

If it be asked why it is that Egyptologists are thus divided on the question at issue, it may be replied that it is occasioned by the difficulty of interpreting some stucco fragments found in Siptah's tomb, and which seem to contradict facts respecting the order of the succession gathered from other monumental sources.

Both Champollion and Lepsius visited this tomb; and both have published detailed accounts of the inscriptions found therein, at least of such of them as were legible.

The interior of the tomb was in a most deplorable condition. Many of the chambers were in utter ruin. Everything about the tomb betokened the purpose of complete demolition. Fortunately, some royal cartouches and portraits and inscriptions had escaped; and all of these are described, with plates, in the two great works of Lepsius and Champollion, which give as fair an account of the tomb and its contents as could be expected.[1]

It would appear, judging from the phenomena of the tomb, that it had been originally constructed for

of the Passover could not have been Mineptah's son; for the son who was his heir, and who in fact succeeded him, had reigned already as a colleague Pharaoh. It is on such grounds as these that it would seem impossible that Mineptah could be the Pharaoh of the Exodus. Maspero explicitly rejects him (see "Histoire," p. 262 et seq.).

[1] Champollion's account is to be found in two magnificent works published by the French Government : (1) "La Description de l'Égypte ; " (2) "Monuments de l'Égypte," etc., with "Notices Descriptives."

Lepsius' great work, a thesaurus for Egyptologists, the "Denkmaeler," was published at the expense of the Prussian Government.

one Tanser, — a queen, who was either at the time, or subsequently became, Siptah's wife; and that thereafter it was adopted as the intended sepulchre for them both. The cartouches of both Tauser and Siptah are clearly legible, with portraits of them both, singly and together.

But there are unmistakable traces of usurpation of the tomb by one Pharaoh, and, as the descriptions and plates of Champollion and Lepsius would show, by more than one Pharaoh.

Now, no difficulty is occasioned by one of these usurpations. All Egyptologists agree as to the usurpation of Siptah's tomb years after by Setnekht, founder of Dynasty XX. It is the other usurpation that occasions perplexity. For it is assuredly perplexing to find, as is alleged, the cartouche of Seti II., if it be his, in Siptah's tomb. It would be perplexing, even on the hypothesis that he really succeeded Siptah; for he had his own tomb in the neighborhood where he was buried, and there would consequently seem to have been no motive for usurping a predecessor's. But it is most perplexing of all, because all other indications, both of the monuments and of the Manetho lists, make Seti II. the immediate and unchallenged successor of his father Mineptah.

Still, Champollion's statement is very explicit. He tells how he found, in certain specified parts of the tomb, fragments of stucco compositions covering the original rock decorations and inscriptions of

Siptah and Tauser, which compositions were in honor
of a Pharaoh who, if Champollion correctly reports
the fragments, would seem to have been Seti II.
He adds, what is certainly confirmatory of his statement, that these stucco compositions (or at least the
cartouches) had been recovered a second time, and
by the Pharaoh who is, without doubt, Setnekht.
Champollion's own conclusion is : " This marks three
epochs or successive conditions of this corridor." [1]

If it is deemed necessary, therefore, to accept this
statement without debate, it would of course oblige
one to regard Seti II. as a successor, not a predecessor, of Siptah, and consequently the Pharaoh of the
Exodus.

And yet, if we accept this conclusion merely from
the data mentioned by Champollion, we are obliged
to go counter to the clear indications of all other
monumental data, which would reverse the order.
Clearly, then, the only way out of the perplexity
arising from the fragments of Siptah's tomb is, if possible, to interpret them so as to harmonize them with
the other monumental data.

Both Chabas and Dr. Eisenlohr believed a mistake
had been made.[2] Chabas, e. g., believed that it was
a mistake of the scribe, who made a blunder in in-
scribing the name, and wrote Seti II. for Setnekht,

---

[1] Notices Descriptives, vol. i. p. 451.

[2] Chabas' " Recherches," p. 115 ; Dr. Eisenlohr's article in " Transactions
of Soc. Bib. Arch.," vol. i.

the two names being very similar; but this would not explain the fact of what would then be two superimpositions by the same Pharaoh on the original inscription.

Dr. Eisenlohr believed that Champollion was mistaken in his facts. As recently as the winter of 1884–1885, Dr. Eisenlohr examined the tomb, and writes: " My visit settled the question whether rightly or wrongly I had asserted that Champollion erred when he said that he had found the name of Seti II. in the tomb of Siptah. I examined all the cartouches of the tomb, and nowhere found Seti II., but continually Setnekht." [1]

It must be added, however, that Lefébure takes up the gauntlet for Champollion, and not only criticises Dr. Eisenlohr's article, but shows how Lepsius' plates seem to corroborate Champollion's statements.[2]

He admits that the cartouche name of Seti II., referred to by Dr. Eisenlohr,[3] " is not found, or at least is no longer found, in Siptah's tomb; " but he differs from Dr. Eisenlohr in that, as he says, " some traces of the second cartouche name of Seti II.[4] are yet seen therein." He refers to a sculptured scene, where

---

[1] Zeitschrift, Part II. for 1885.

[2] Idem, Part IV. for 1885.  In Part I. (1886), p. 40, Dr. Eisenlohr replies to Lefébure's strictures, maintaining his original position.

[3] Viz., " Ra user *cheperu* meramen " (Fig. 8), ; i. e., " the sun, lord of creation, beloved of Amen."

[4] Viz., " Seti merenptah " (Fig. 3) ; i. e., " Seti, beloved of Ptah."

Siptah is represented as offering the symbol of the goddess Ma[1] to Isis, and to the fact that in one of

  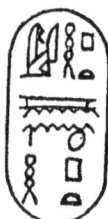  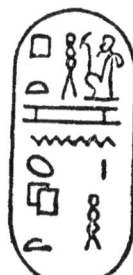

Fig. 3.    Fig. 4.    Fig 5.    Fig. 6.    Fig. 7.

Siptah's cartouches[2] in the scene two other stucco letters, viz., ⌀ and ∿ (i. e., "a" and "n") can be distinguished, disposed as in Fig. 4, in the shield at just the places where the corresponding letters in the name of Seti II. (Fig. 3) would be found.

He also draws attention to the fact that Lepsius[3] saw some superimposed stucco fragments (see Fig. 5) on a Siptah cartouche. There was in this instance a reduplication of the letter ⌀, almost confounded with the symbol for Ptah[4] of Siptah's name (compare Figs. 6 and 7). This would naturally suggest

---

[1] I. e., the goddess of Justice and Truth.

[2] Viz., "Ptah meren Siptah" (Fig. 6); i. e., "Siptah, beloved of Ptah."

[3] Denkmaeler, III., Pl. 201, b.

[4] In cutting cartouches the characters were made to look to the right or left, as symmetry required. The two cartouches, e. g., Figs. 5 and 6 (as cut on the rock), were the very same, except that the position of the letters is reversed, because Fig. 5 was on the left side and Fig. 6 on the right side of a Siptah portrait, and all looked toward him. Thus understood, the argument based on the stucco fragments of the first usurpation may be somewhat clearer.

the reduplicated ⟨ in the name of Seti II. (Fig. 3).
Further, Lepsius noted,[1] in another instance, a letter ☐ (i. e., " p "), strangely enough mixed up (see
Fig. 7) with the same letter of Siptah's name (compare Figs. 5 and 6); and he adds that of all the
known Pharaohs concerned, it is only in the name of
Seti II. (Fig. 3) that these several letters appear in
a cartouche in that position.  And so Lefébure concludes that " one must see in the fragments the
name of Seti II."

He further argues that " this statement and that
of Champollion confirm and mutually support each
other ; for if one of the names of Seti II. is still
found in the first corridor, it is not surprising that
Champollion should have found and copied the other
in the second corridor, as he alleges."

He adds : " It is useless to suppose, as Chabas does,
a scribe's error, that substituted the beetle 🪲 in the
name of Seti II. (Fig. 8) for the crown ⚷, in the

same position in Setnekht's name
(Fig. 9); for the proper name of
Setnekht, which occurs throughout the tomb frequently, is every-
where written as in Fig. 9, and
the name referred to by Cham-

Fig. 8.   Fig. 9.

pollion (Fig. 8) is much shorter." [2]

[1] Denkmaeler, III. Pl. 201, a.

[2] While the two names are very similar, they differ in two particulars
(1) In the first clause one has a beetle and the other a crown (or, as some

He concludes: "If one wishes to know who reigned first, Seti II. or Siptah, he has but to examine on the spot which cartouche was written over the other."

Now, if this seems decisive of the question at issue, it may be added that there are some things to be said on the other side. For there are other monumental indications that are indisputable and equally decisive, that would forbid the acceptance of Lefébure's conclusion. And it may be further stated that there is a possible explanation, which may serve to harmonize the facts and thus help to determine the problem.

First of all, both Manetho and the monuments, with the single exception that is so perplexing, make Seti II. the immediate successor of his father; Mineptah. All the Manetho lists, e. g., indicate this as the succession, and they all end the Dynasty strangely enough with "Thuoris" (i. e., Tauser), Siptah's queen. To be sure, Eusebius makes Tauser a king, and identifies her (or him) with "Homer's Polybus, husband

explain it, a rising sun) ; so that the one reads "Ra user *cheperu*" (" Ra, lord of creation "), instead of "Ra user *Khau*" (" Ra, lord of lords," — lit., "of rising suns or crowns "). (2) The one inserts and the other omits a clause frequently used in cartouches, — viz., " Sotep en Ra "(" chosen of Ra "). The remaining clause is the same in each, — "miamen " (" beloved of Amen "). The omission in Fig. 8 of the second clause of Fig. 9 would occasion no difficulty, were there no other difference between the two. It would be simply a shorter form of the name. But the substitution of a beetle in the one for the rising sun of the other creates a far more serious difficulty, which requires special pleading to surmount. Chabas' surmise that the substitution was a scribe's mistake is what Lefébure rightly refuses to allow. Besides, it does not remove the difficulty ; for were it allowed, it would then follow that Setnekht covered over his own cartouche, which would need explanation.

of Aleandra;" but this was a blunder. It is really an instance of misplacement; for there was another "Thuoris" in Dynasty XXI.,[1] who is connected there with the identical tradition as Homer's Polybus, etc. At any rate, the monuments settle it that the Tanser of Dynasty XIX. was a queen. Why Queen Tauser's name should have been inserted in all the Manetho lists as ending the Dynasty, instead of her husband's, it is impossible to say. One may only conjecture. Still, it is evident that the Manetho lists, without exception, would make the order of succession to be Seti II., Amenmes, and Siptah (as Tauser's husband).

Then, secondly, the monumental indications are equally clear. A number of monuments, to begin with, represent this Seti II. as crown prince; e. g., there is a sitting statue of Mineptah at Boulak, on the left side of which Seti II. is represented with the titles of royal son and heir. Some literary works were dedicated to him while yet crown prince, showing that he had literary tastes and was considered a patron of learning. It is not to be forgotten that his father was advanced in years when he became a Pharaoh; so that it is probable that Seti himself while crown prince was no longer young. It is certain, moreover, that he was associated with his father on the throne, for the associated cartouches of the two are found in a rock temple excavated by

---

[1] See p. 18 of the "Tables," in Lepsius' "Königsbuch."

Mineptah at Sourarieh.[1] Further, the few remains of his short sole reign that have survived indicate no political complications as accompanying his accession, and no disturbance of the ordinary routine of a time of peace. The city of Rameses, added to by Mineptah, was still occupied under Seti II. as an important point and a royal residence. It was there, indeed, that he celebrated a special feast in honor of his grandfather, who had founded the cult. He still kept up the usual communications with the frontier garrisons, and maintained the desert wells.[2] The beginning of his reign, therefore, was peaceful, whatever its end was. Its close is unknown. It is only known that it was a short reign ; for he died not only before his tomb was finished, but when most of its galleries and halls had been simply hewn out of the rock and left in the rough. His granite sarcophagus was found inside with its cover, but in an unusual place, — in the very first corridor, which itself was not yet completed, even the floor being still rough, as though he had been buried therein (and hastily) soon after its commencement. Only his second year has been yielded by the monuments ; though some would assign him four years, — meaning of course for his sole reign. No information has reached modern times respecting his family, unless

---

[1] Chabas' Recherches, p. 116.

[2] Idem, p. 123, where there is a translation of a curious document referring to this.

a Manetho tradition, soon to be mentioned, can be referred to him. At any rate, according to these monumental indications, the son succeeded to the father and without a challenge. Whether he was literally Mineptah's "first-born" cannot of course be affirmed or denied. But the " first-born of Pharaoh that sitteth upon his throne " (Gen. xi. 5), who was destroyed on the eve of the Exodus, could not have been Seti II., for this latter prince *survived to succeed his father.* The fact of itself would seem to exclude Mineptah as a possible Exodus Pharaoh.[1]

These monumental arguments, as they may be called, are indeed so strong that were it not for the perplexing fragments in Siptah's tomb, there could be no doubt whatever as to the order of the succession. The question may therefore well suggest itself, Is there any possible hypothesis that can justify one in accepting the clear indications of the monuments referred to and at the same time explain the tomb fragments ?  The period is one concerning which so little is actually known that conjecture is as yet the only resource in trying to solve the problem.  There are two items in the count, however, that seem to be matters of fact, and which, taken together, suggest a possible explanation of the phenomena, both of the tomb and of the other monu-

---

[1] This is the only hint in the Hebrew story, if it be so interpreted, that there was an associated Pharaoh on the throne when Moses had his memorable interviews.  The bearing of this hint on Siptah's case will be seen in the sequel.

ments, — viz., (1) that there was at the time another
Seti, a prince who cannot be identified with either
Seti II. or Setnekht; and (2) that in some way
Siptah owed a good deal to Queen Tauser.

There is monumental evidence, e. g.,[1] that there
was a Seti who was a " Prince of Cush " and who
bore numerous other titles, proving that he was at
least a scion of the royal house. He was, moreover,
not only contemporary with Siptah, but acted as
a courtier under him. It is never said nor intimated
that he was Siptah's son. No son of Siptah is ever
mentioned. In fact, nothing further is known of
him. He simply appears on two monuments, — one
found at the island of Sehel and the other at Assouan,
— and in the pictures is represented as a youth rendering homage to Siptah, who is crowned. As he bore
the titles referred to and occupied the usual position
of a prince of the blood, it may be inferred that he
had some claim to the succession. Who was he ?

Now, curiously enough, there is a Manetho tradition that one of the Mineptahs of this Dynasty,
on occasion arising, sent his son Sethos, but a child
of five years, into Ethiopia for safety, and himself
fled thither subsequently.[2] This Mineptah could
not very well have been the Mineptah who was father to Seti II., — for, as Chabas has shown, he died
in peace and was peacefully succeeded by his son;

---

[1] Chabas' Recherches, p. 115.
[2] Josephus' Contra Apionem, lib. i.

nay, the son had been already associated with the
father before he died.    Also the very young age
of the child Sethos of the tradition could scarcely
be harmonized with the relative ages of Mineptah
and Seti II., as they are ordinarily conceived.    But
Seti II. himself was also a " Mineptah," and could
easily enough have had a son named Seti, who, as
hereditary prince, would be " Prince of Cush," etc.
Further, while there is monumental evidence that
the reign of Seti II. began peacefully, there is evidence that would point to its having been suddenly
cut short; so that it is altogether probable that his
reign ended disastrously.    There is monumental evidence, indeed, of some trouble, — in truth, evidence
that points to even the kind of trouble that brought
his rule to an end.    There is a large sitting statue
of Seti II., now in the British Museum, bearing his
cartouches in three places; but the syllable " Set "
(it is the figure of the god Set 𓊖 ) is in all three
places chiselled out.    This of itself points to the
jealousies of the Theban priests, who were irritated,
as is known, that the successor to the first Rameses
should call himself a Seti.    In fact, they refused to
recognize the name, and called him after Osiris instead.    They were doubtless still more irritated that
the first Mineptah's son should repeat the hated
name, and yet more so that now, if the hypothesis
be accepted, the second Seti should give the same

name to his heir. This jealousy, coupled with the inevitable intrigues of a court made up of a multitude of descendants of the great Rameses, all claiming some status in the royal house, would be sure to make the Theban priests all the more ready to lend their countenance and support to any royal prince, with a shadow of a claim to the throne, who would identify himself with their theological predilections. From this point of view it is certainly, then, more than a coincidence that the only possible contestant of Seti II., revealed by the monuments of the period, should be the man, whoever he was, who, both by the name he assumed and the legend he put in his cartouche, would suggest a religious plea for his recognition. He styled himself "*Amen*mes, Prince of Thebes."

It follows that the Seti who was a prince of the blood and afterwards Siptah's courtier may well enough have been a son of Seti II. Mineptah, the child Sethos of the tradition, sent to Ethiopia for safety amid the troubles that harassed the close of his father's reign.

He could not have been the future Setnekht of Dynasty XX.; for in the "Great Harris Papyrus" Rameses III. puts forth on behalf of his father no claim to royal heirship. It is not said that Setnekht was established on his father's throne, but that "the gods established him on their own seat."[1] Surely,

---

[1] Records of the Past, vol. viii. p. 46.

had such been the fact, Rameses III. would not have failed to claim for his father sonship to one of the Dynasty XIX. Pharaohs. That he does not, shows that Setnekht was simply a leader, possibly allied to the royal house, who seized his chance and having quelled anarchy took a royal name that seemed at least to keep up the traditions. And the name he took is itself very suggestive. It is certainly worthy of notice that the founder of Dynasty XX., in choosing his throne name, should have selected that of " Seti." Is it to be believed that he would have chosen this name had Seti II. been the Pharaoh with whom the Dynasty closed in such disaster? Would the man who put an end to the period of anarchy occasioned by the disaster to which the Harris Papyrus refers have taken the name of the Pharaoh who inaugurated it? And is there not an incidental proof, therefore, in the very name Setnekht assumed, that Seti II. did not end the Dynasty? The sequel will show, moreover, that in choosing Seti as a name the founder of Dynasty XX., who was doubtless desirons of keeping up a connection with the past, made a wise choice of a name.

Who Amenmes was, no one can say with certainty. The monuments simply point to him as the man who contested with Seti II. the sovereignty of Egypt. He called himself in his cartouche " Prince of Thebes," and it is evident that his reign was recognized by the Theban priests. He may have

been one of the many grandsons of Rameses II.,
probably a son of an older brother of Mineptah's.
Political ambition would doubtless characterize such
a man, living as he would amid the conspiracies of a
court. He would be sure to see his chance, amid
the religious animosities of the day, to play a rôle
as the champion of " Amen " and the old-time dogmas, in opposition to the " Set " worshippers. It is
also possible, if the Manetho tradition can be trusted,
that he saw a further opportunity in the extreme
youth of the heir of Seti II. It is undoubtedly
possible to fit in these suppositions with the sure
monumental indications of the period. The " Seti,
Prince of Cush," of the monuments could easily
enough be the young son of Seti II., who at the out-
break of hostilities between his father and Amenmes
was sent for safety to Ethiopian friends, and was
thus far away when his father's reign came suddenly
to an end. It is but needful to suppose that at his
father's death the " Prince of Cush " was for the
time being thrust aside, to make clear what was
probably the rest of the story. Amenmes for the
time reigned as a veritable Pharaoh, recognized as
such by the priests, and long enough to build a tomb
in the king's valley.

It is evident, however, that Amenmes did not rule
with an undisputed sway ; for it was undoubtedly
contested, — notably by Siptah.

Siptah at least reached the throne only after a

struggle with some pretender or usurper; for the monuments mention that with the help of Baï, who became his Premier, he was at length, as he affirms, " established on his father's throne, and *after silencing a lie.*" [1]

Who his royal father could have been, can only be conjectured. There is a chapel at Silsilis, specially consecrated to Mineptah, whose legends decorate the door and are also found inside, where they are associated with the cartouches of his son Seti II.[2] Curiously, Siptah is also found there, represented as in his tomb, in the act of offering the symbol of " Ma " (or " justice ") to Amen-Ra. The association of the cartouches of the three in this little chapel would certainly show a family connection to have existed between Mineptah, Mineptah Seti II., and Mineptah Siptah, — a connection which would be suggested further by the fact that they were all three Mineptahs. The temple scene certainly claims some connection between the three. It is, in fact, perfectly possible that he, as well as Seti II., may have been a son of Mineptah. He may have been a younger brother, therefore, of Seti II., who amid the conspiracies that ended his brother's reign and the enforced absence of the still young prince Seti, his nephew, or his minority, deemed himself possessed of a valid claim to his father's throne, but

---

[1] Chabas' Recherches, p. 128.
[2] Idem, p. 81.

found himself for a time unable to dispossess Amen-mes, who had obtained Theban recognition.

Moreover, all Egyptologists agree in looking on Siptah, whatever his personal claim may have been, as not so unquestionably a Pharaoh as to need no support for his claim; and all of them agree in regarding his marriage with Queen Tauser as a political move. And there are indications that this was so.

Siptah's tomb, e. g., as has been stated, seems to have been at first made, not by him nor for him, but for the queen. There are indisputable evidences of enlargement and alterations, which belong to their own era and not to the period of usurpation. There is good reason, therefore, for believing that after Siptah married Tauser, rather than build a new one, the old tomb designed for her was simply altered so as to make it serve for them both.

Who Tauser was, is unknown. She may have been a queen-dowager, and with special rights also as the daughter of a Pharaoh. It is possible for her to have been the Queen of Seti II. and the mother of the young "Prince of Cush," who, after her husband's death, kept up in the North a sort of regency, notwithstanding the success of Amenmes in the South; for no indication has been met of the latter's presence in the North.

As such, she may have found in Siptah, her husband's brother and her child's uncle, according to the hypothesis, one to espouse her cause as against Amenmes. There would be nothing improbable, either, in her marrying the man who was at length successful in overthrowing the rival of her house, and even in agreeing, as a choice between evils, to a compromise as to the throne, — viz., that Siptah during the minority of her son should reign jointly with herself, with the understanding that the young " Prince of Cush, Seti," was to be his successor.

In this way Siptah would add to his own claim to the throne (as the surviving son of his father) — a claim which could be contested — the claim he could make as the husband of Queen Tauser. He would therefore simply hold in abeyance during a minority the succession of Prince Seti, the rightful heir. Whatever hypothesis, however, be adopted, it is admitted by all that in some way Siptah owed much to his queen. The tomb was beyond a doubt originally excavated for her. At the entrance, where one always looks for the name of the tomb's builder, there are some fragments of stucco with which the rock was invested. On the fillet of the doorway are to be found the traces of two successive pictures, the more ancient sculptured on the stone itself and containing only Tauser's legend as a queen. On the jambs of the doorway, also sculptured on the rock, is seen the beginning of an inscription to the same queen, beginning with the words "hereditary daughter . . . exalted . . ." She was therefore unquestionably a queen in her own right.[1] It was not until Siptah was associated with her that the alterations and enlargements were made, and a few portraits of the two sculptured together. While Tauser is met in inscriptions and portraits every-where through the tomb, except in the additions made by Setnekht, Siptah himself is rarely met therein.

It is certainly true, therefore, putting all the facts together, that the queen in some way was more a queen than was Siptah a king. This may serve to explain why it is that in the Manetho lists Queen Tauser ends Dynasty XIX., rather than Siptah, her husband. According to Egyptian usage, a man's marriage with a queen, who was such in her own right, did not make him a legitimate Pharaoh, had he no other claim to the throne. Their common children derived from the marriage the right of suc-cession, though not from the father, but from the mother. In this particular case the young "Prince Seti" would be regarded as hereditary prince, both by right and by agreement, and consequently Sip-tah's "first-born" would only rightfully come next in the succession. To be sure, all such arrangements would be certain to produce jealousies and family dissensions; and it can be understood how on the death of the queen the agreement might be ignored, and Siptah claim the throne for himself not only,

---

[1] Notices Descriptives, vol. i. p. 448.

but set aside the son of his wife, the rightful heir, and claim the succession for his own son. Some such state of things would explain how peculiarly striking a judgment it would appear to Pharaoh that slew his " first-born " and yet allowed a foster-child to survive.

What the throne names of the young Prince Seti may have been, when he attempted to succeed Siptah, is of course pure conjecture. On the monuments that associate him with Siptah he is simply "Seti, Prince of Cush," with other titles, such as were borne by a hereditary prince ; and no one, therefore, can tell whether his throne names, if known, would satisfy the conditions mentioned by Champollion and Lepsius respecting the first usurper of Siptah's tomb. And yet one can understand how such a prince, the victim of so many intrigues, whose rights had been so long held in abeyance, first by Amenmes and then by Siptah himself, albeit the latter at first pretended to recognize and befriend him, would take the first chance after Siptah was swept away to resent his own wrongs by covering Siptah's cartouches with his own.

It would be perfectly natural, moreover, for such a prince to adopt for his cartouches names as like his father's as possible. It is but needful to suppose that for the one he took the family name (which he bore indeed as Prince), so that his first cartouche would be identical with that of his father and with that of the first Seti,[1] in order adequately to explain the perplexing fragments of Fig. 4. Then, if it be supposed that for his other name he took the first part of his father's second cartouche, and for distinction's sake simply changed the latter half, so that his second cartouche would read "Ra user cheperu *mer en ptah*," instead of his father's "Ra user cheperu *mer amen*," this would also adequately explain the perplexing fragments of Figs. 5 and 7, particularly that ▫ ("p"), mixed up with another "p" of Fig. 7. It would also explain the second ᴀᴀᴀ ("n") observable in Fig. 5.[2]

In this way the argument derived from the fragmentary cartouches of the first usurper of Siptah's tomb against the immediate succession of Seti II. to his father Mineptah, so explicitly certified to by all other monuments, entirely loses its force.

It is altogether likely, therefore, that the fragments that have occasioned so much perplexity refer to another Pharaoh than Seti II., — a Pharaoh who may reasonably enough be identified as the monumental "Seti, Prince of Cush," who (1) was

---

[1] His first cartouche would be the same as Fig. 3. This was not unusual. The first cartouches, e. g, of all four Amenemhats of Dynasty XII. were identical.

[2] This supposition also would involve no unusual procedure. In the second cartouches, e. g., of all four Thothmes of Dynasty XVIII., there is a very slight alteration made, for distinction's sake, in the form of the legend, the sentiment remaining virtually the same. Thus in that of Thothmes III. we read "Ra men cheper," and in that of Thothmes IV. is found simply the plural of the same, "Ra men cheperu." It cannot be said, therefore, that either supposition of the text is impossible, or even improbable.

certainly a courtier under Siptah, (2) who could easily
have been a young son and rightful heir of Seti II.,
and (3) who may easily enough have attempted at
least to succeed Siptah. For if Siptah was the Pharaoh after whom came anarchy, — or, as the event
has been understood in these lectures, the Exodus
Pharaoh, — it can easily have been after the death of
Siptah's "first-born," and after the disaster which,
as the Bible suggests, overtook him and his, that a
surviving rightful heir should have attempted for a
while, at least in the South, whither he had doubtless
fled, to stem the tide of confusion that ensued, and
even have time to dishonor the empty tomb, and yet
himself be soon swept out of sight amid the anarchy
that overwhelmed the country.

To be sure, all this is purely hypothetical; but it
certainly does in a reasonable way harmonize the
known facts of the monuments with the order of
succession that may be called traditional. It explains, however inadequately in the opinion of some,
the only doubt as to the order of succession, occasioned by Siptah's tomb. Rather than agree with
Chabas or Eisenlohr, that Lepsius and Champollion
blundered in their transcriptions and statements, or
even that a scribe blundered in copying a very similar name, one might be willing to adopt any hypothesis that may remove the perplexity occasioned
by the tomb's phenomena. When every other monumental indication justifies a certain order of the

succession, some explanation of the single exception
may be sought. Besides, if the traditional order
must be upset by the single exception, the necessity would remain to explain in some satisfactory
way the monumental indications that intimate an
unchallenged succession by Seti II. to his father's
throne.

Such is the state of the evidence, on account of
which some Egyptologists end Dynasty XIX. with
Seti II., others with Siptah. The issue at present,
consequently, is uncertain, and the problem unsolved.
It will be seen, however, that the problem has been
brought in these last days within narrower limits.
It may be claimed with some degree of confidence
respecting the Exodus Pharaoh, that on the one
hand he was not Mineptah, the son of Rameses II.,
and that, on the other hand, he was either Mineptah
Seti II. or Mineptah Siptah. Both of these Pharaohs ruled all Egypt, and either of them would
abundantly satisfy the Bible portraiture of the man
who dared to withstand God; though, apart from
the traditional order which would point to Siptah
as the man, his history of conflict issuing in victory
could readily have so far elated him as to lead him
to believe that he could succeed against the God
of the Hebrews.

Summing up the case as respects Siptah, (1) he
was probably the last Pharaoh of Dynasty XIX.;
(2) he was a " Mineptah," thus satisfying the tradi-

tion that affirms the Exodus Pharaoh to have been such; (3) his tomb proved to be a tomb that could be usurped, twice usurped, — in the first instance by one " Seti," whoever he was; and subsequently by Setnekht, founder of Dynasty XX. There is no evidence that the former occupied it; but the latter did. It is interesting, however, to know that while Setnekht was buried therein, he was not buried in Siptah's sepulchral hall. No trace of Siptah's burial in the tomb has ever been found. The lid of Setnekht's sarcophagus was found in the second sepulchral hall, but nothing that would indicate Siptah's burial in his tomb. The two usurpations would indeed seem to settle that point. Nevertheless, while usurping the tomb, Setnekht resorted to a device that is unique in tomb architecture, — an added second sepulchral chamber, separated from the original funeral hall by two long corridors, as though, as Champollion says,[1] for some reason he did not wish to lie in Siptah's chamber. It was not that the tomb was not large enough; for it is the third in size of all the known kings' tombs, and one of rare magnificence. The facts are so novel that one cannot help conjecturing some motive for the additions. Does not it seem to intimate that when Setnekht reached the throne, he found an empty tomb all ready to hand, and so usurped it, simply transforming it to suit his own purposes? But while

[1] Notices Descriptives, vol. i. p. 459.

he could cover over with stucco the old cartouches, as though their owner, because the author of national disasters, deserved to be so disgraced, he could not bring himself to lie where Siptah was to have laid, and so made for himself his own death-chamber.

# ESSAY

## "APERIU" AND THE "HEBREWS."

---

THERE are still two opinions about the propriety of regarding the proper name ⟨hieroglyphs⟩ "Aperiu" or "Aperu" of the monuments as the proper name "Hebrews" of Holy Scripture. Those who disallow the identification allege that there are two difficulties in the way, one philological and the other historical.

The philological difficulty is the presence in "Aperiu" of a ▫ )" p ") instead of the ⟨glyph⟩ (" b ") that, as Brugsch says,[1] one would expect to find.

But to this objection several considerations may be urged : —

(1) The precise phonetic value of the two hieroglyphs in dispute still remains uncertain. And this is to a degree true even of the letter ב of the Hebrew name.[2] To judge from some Greek transcriptions of

---

[1] Dict. Géog., p. 113.

[2] It is generally stated as "bh," or as equivalent to the English " v," just as the modern Greeks sound their β. With a daghesh בּ, the aspirate is removed.

proper names containing the ◨, as, e. g., Mine*ph*-
tah and Si*ph*tah instead of Mine*p*tah and Si*p*tah,
the ◨ was sounded more like the Greek "ph"
than " P," and the former of these was most probably more like the sound of the Hebrew ב than
was that of the hieroglyph 𝍌 commonly considered
as "b."

(2) The "b" and "P" are closely related sounds.
They are both consonantal "mutes," and in Greek belonged to the same general class of P sounds.   The
three Greek letters π, β, φ, were simply the same
P mute, only differentiated as smooth, middle, and
aspirated, according to the measure of exertion used
in the pronunciation.

(3) There was, as a matter of fact, no absolute
uniformity in the transcriptions of foreign names.
This may be illustrated by the case of another "p"
hieroglyph; for the Egyptian script was rich in
many signs for the same letter.   This originated
most probably in the fact that the signs were the
first picture letters of words beginning with the same
sound.   They may be regarded as alphabetic equiv-
aleuts, and were used as variants.   In this way there
were many "p" signs.   There was, e. g., a sign ▭,
which was just as much a "p" as was the sign ◨ in
"Aperiu."   Now, this sign ▭, which forms an element of so many proper names, is transcribed into
Greek by all three forms of the P mute.   It is, e. g.,
the initial letter in the original of all three of the

words transcribed into Greek as *P*atoumos, *B*ousiris, and *Ph*araoh. And if this is true of one so-called " p," why should it not be equally true of the others ? And if it is true of Greek, why should it not be of Hebrew transcriptions ? In fact, " A*p*eriu," for the Pentateuchal " He*b*rews," does not stand quite alone. Chabas (in " Mélanges Égyptol. ' vol. i. p. 48) gives another instance where the ב in a Hebrew word (Khore*b*) is transliterated into Egyptian by a ▢ instead of a 𝕁

(4) There are indications in the Egyptian script itself that the " P " and " b " were, to a degree at least, interchangeable. Brugsch (in " Dict. Hiérog.," vol. ii. p. 365) shows, e. g., that the sound of " b " was modified by what are known as phonetic equiv. alents, which served as determinatives of sound. Now, curiously enough, one of the phonetic determi- natives that sometimes follows 𝕁 (" b ") is another of the signs for " p," viz., 🦅. This would certainly intimate, in view of the office of the phonetic deter- minative, that the 𝕁 (" b ") could be sometimes sounded as 🦅, and, of course, vice versa.

It is therefore very probable that in Egyptian, as in other languages, the " p " and " b " signs were not only closely related, but, as variant names would show, not so precisely discriminated on all occasions as some have imagined. Instead therefore of con- cluding, as some have done, from finding a ▢ instead of a ∬ in the monumental "Aperiu," that it could not have been intended as a transcription of the Hebrew word for "Hebrews," it would probably be more correct to conclude that the ם, better than a ∬ would have done, represented the sound which the Egyptian scribes heard when the Hebrews pronounced their national name.

The historical objection raised to the identification is twofold, — (1) that the monumental name can be referred to another people than the Hebrews; (2) that "Aperiu" are met in reigns subsequent to the Exodus.

Respecting the first form of the objection, Brugsch, e. g., identifies them as descendants of some prisoners brought back from Syria by Thothmes III., and described as coming from two towns, each called "Aper."

The name of the two towns "Aper" is found on a Karnak pylon, but without any further allusion to its locale than that, like all the rest, they were Syrian towns.[1] The name "Aperu" itself is met but once previous to the time of Dynasty XIX. It was found on the back of a papyrus belonging to Thothmes' day, and in a single clause where it is said, "Let one of the *Aperu* ride out," as though they were

---

[1] Brugsch's "History," vol. i. p. 350; Mariette's "Les listes géog. des Pylones de Karnak;" Maspero in "Trans. Vict. Instit.," vol. xx., "on the geographical names of the list of Thothmes III. which may be referred to Galilee."

"knights, who mounted their horses at the king's command."[1]　It is of course possible that these knights were the war prisoners from the "Aper" towns, who, as the Karnak inscription says, like the prisoners from the other towns, were assigned as servants to the Theban temples. But this is not certain. They are nowhere again mentioned, and it is therefore gratuitous to affirm that the "Aperiu" met on the Dynasty XIX. monuments (some two centuries later) were their descendants.

The later "Aperiu" are found in Lower, not in Upper Egypt; and they are described not as temple servants or warrior knights, but as slaves condemned to the quarry and to bear burdens.

A yet more serious objection to their being the same is found in the Egyptian script itself, which by using a different determinative with the word as it is found in the two eras, would suggest them to have been different peoples.

The earlier "Aperu" is written with the determinative ⛭, which is not ethnic, but, as Brugsch says, conveys the idea of smallness or youth.

The later "Aperiu" is always written with the determinative ⎞, which is the conventional symbol of a foreign people. Chabas remarks that there is an Egyptian word " aper," which means " to provide, to fortify;" but, as he says, " this meaning is not

---

[1] See Mr. Goodwin in " Trans. Soc. Bib. Arch.," vol. iii. p. 342.

ethnic; where it is found with the determinative of a foreign people, there we have to do."[1]

The later " Aperiu," first met in Dynasty XIX., do certainly, as described on the monuments, fit in most admirably with the story of the Hebrews, as to era, locale, and occupation.

Thus the Bible tells how the Hebrews built Pithom and Ramses as fortified magazines for Pharaoh. Now, the former has been discovered; and monuments recovered thence prove that the town unearthed was a fortified store-city, and owed its foundation to Rameses II. The identification in this case of the Hebrews as the builders of Rameses' " Pithom " is complete. The other town " Ramses " has not yet been found, possibly because in this case explorers have been looking for it as a separate town, whereas in all probability this store-city was not really a separate town, but an extension or addition to an old town. It is undoubtedly true, according to a papyrus,[2] that the same Pharaoh who built Pithom employed the " Aperiu " in making an important addition to his capital of a grand fortress-tower, which is called therein " the tower of Ramses Miamen." In the case of the fortress " Ramses," therefore, built by command of Rameses II., it was the " Aperiu " that built it.

---

[1] Recherches, p. 104.

[2] Pap. Leyden, I. 349, line 7; Chabas' Recherches, p. 102, and his Mélanges, vol. i. p. 49.

Is it possible, then, putting these indications together, any longer to disallow the identification? For it would certainly be a remarkable circumstance, one quite as difficult to accept as the identification proposed, if we are to believe that there were living in the very same era and in the very same locale, nay, side by side, two peoples called (writing their two names as the supposition would require) "Aperiu" and "Aberin," — both foreign peoples reduced to servitude, and both doing the very same work; nay more, both contributing to the construction of the store-fortress "Ramses" of Rameses II. Must this be believed? If the identification of the "Khita" and the "Hittites," of "Thuku" and "Succoth," so long debated, is now generally allowed, why should that of the "Aperiu" and the "Hebrews" be disallowed?

It has been urged further as a difficulty, that a band of "Aperiu," 2,083 strong, is mentioned in the time of Rameses III., and another band of 800 in the time of Rameses IV., — i. e., subsequent to the Exodus.[1] They are also indicated as foreigners, and they are located in the old quarries of the Rameses II. "Aperiu," not far from the Gulf of Suez.[2]

Chabas regarded them as mercenaries who elected to remain after the Exodus; though it would be

---

[1] Brugsch's History, vol. ii. p. 129; Speaker's Commentary, vol. i. p. 467.
[2] Brugsch's Dict. Géog., p. 115.

difficult to explain, as Canon Cook suggests, why they should have wished or dared to stay, and why their presence would be tolerated after the Exodus.

But, curiously enough, those of Rameses III. are indicated by two determinatives, — one, the usual determinative for foreigners; the other is that of a leg in a trap, the meaning of which is obvious. They were probably prisoners forwarded by some garrison commander of Rameses III., who assisted the inhabitants of the land in some conflict with the Hebrews during the earlier period of their Palestine conquest.

In the case of the 800 "Aperiu" of Rameses IV. the group is written not only with the general determinative for foreigners, but with a group representing bowmen, which would clearly indicate that those "Aperiu" were foreign bowmen taken prisoners, most probably in a skirmish. The fact, in connection with the lapse of time in this case, would show that the conquerors of Palestine, whence doubtless they came, had become a military people. Nothing would be more natural than to send these "Hebrew" prisoners to the very place associated with their fathers, and to the same dreaded toil.

Summing up the argument, it may be said that even if the identification may not be yet as decisive as one could wish, it is certainly possible; nay more, probable.

The sacred writer tells us that his people were called "Hebrews." The monuments seem to show that Pharaoh and the Egyptians wrote of them as "Aperiu." One must here, as elsewhere, simply wait for the complete justification of the identification that is sure to come.

www.ingramcontent.com/pod-product-compliance
Lightning Source LLC
Chambersburg PA
CBHW051433270326
41935CB00018B/1815